**Anticipate
Your Future Hope,
Your Eternal Home,
Your Daily Reality**

HEAVEN AWAIT

MICHAEL YOUSSEF

TYNDALE
MOMENTUM®

A Tyndale nonfiction imprint

Visit Tyndale online at tyndale.com.

Visit Tyndale Momentum online at tyndalemomentum.com.

Tyndale, Tyndale's quill logo, *Tyndale Momentum*, and the Tyndale Momentum logo are registered trademarks of Tyndale House Ministries. Tyndale Momentum is a nonfiction imprint of Tyndale House Publishers, Carol Stream, Illinois.

Heaven Awaits: Anticipate Your Future Hope, Your Eternal Home, Your Daily Reality

Published in association with Don Gates of the literary agency The Gates Group; www.the-gates-group.com.

For information about special discounts for bulk purchases, please contact Tyndale House Publishers at csresponse@tyndale.com, or call 1-855-277-9400.

Library of Congress Cataloging-in-Publication Data

A catalog record for this book is available from the Library of Congress.

ISBN 978-1-4964-8633-2

Printed in the United States of America

30	29	28	27	26	25	24
7	6	5	4	3	2	1

Contents

Introduction

INVESTING IN ETERNITY

LIKE MILLIONS OF PEOPLE from around the world, I came to America to discover a new life. Nearly fifty years later, I clearly remember the hours my wife, Elizabeth, and I spent preparing to move to the US. We pored over books and magazines, searching out every detail we could find about this nation we would soon call home.

The hours we spent learning about America were well-invested. Soon after we stepped off the plane in Los Angeles, we discovered how different the US is from any other place we had lived before. We found ourselves dealing with a new currency, a new climate, new forms of housing and transportation, a new education system, and most of all, new political freedoms. Every experience was fresh, surprising, and exciting.

The way Elizabeth and I prepared ourselves for coming to America is the way all Christians should prepare for going to Heaven. We should look forward to Heaven with excitement and anticipation. We should want to read everything and learn everything we can about our future eternal home.

Yet I find that few Christians make any serious preparations for Heaven. We spend most of our time planning our next vacation or preparing for retirement. We seldom give any thought to eternity.

Our earthly business can often seem so pressing that we tell ourselves, "I really don't have any time to think about Heaven today. Maybe tomorrow or next week." But our eternal future is one of the most foundational truths of the Christian faith.

If you have placed your trust in Jesus Christ, your place in Heaven is assured. Why wouldn't you want to know everything you can about what it will be like? Why wouldn't you want to study the beauty, benefits, and blessings of your eternal home?

Heaven is a real place. It exists right now. Jesus said, "My Father's house has many rooms; if that were not so, would I have told you that I am going there to prepare a place for you? And if I go and prepare a place for you, I will come back and take you to be with me that you also may be where I am" (John 14:2-3).

The apostle Paul longed so intensely for Heaven that he confessed he only continued his earthly ministry out of a sense of duty. He truly wished he could leave this earthly life and join his Lord in Heaven. He confessed, "I am torn between the two: I desire to depart and be with Christ, which is better by far; but it is more necessary for you that I remain in the body" (Philippians 1:23-24).

In 2 Corinthians 12:2, Paul talks about "a man in Christ who fourteen years ago was caught up" into Heaven. Bible scholars agree that Paul was obliquely speaking of himself. He had actually seen Heaven firsthand, though he adds, "Whether it was in the body or out of the body I do not know—God knows." Because Paul had experienced Heaven in a deeply personal (though temporary) way, he couldn't wait to be in Heaven forever.

In this earthly life, we cannot know the same privilege Paul knew of being taken up for a direct experience of Heaven. Yet we can catch a glimpse and a foretaste of Heaven through the Bible. The more we learn about Heaven from God's Word, the more real it will be to us—and the more we will long to be there with Jesus.

Heaven is the fulfillment of all our greatest spiritual longings. As Solomon wrote at the height of his wisdom, God "set eternity in the human heart; yet no one can fathom what God has done from beginning to end" (Ecclesiastes 3:11).

My goal in this book is to stir in your heart a hunger for eternity; to fill your mind with a knowledge of all the wonders and glories that await you in Heaven; and energize you to live each day in light of the reality of Heaven. You have no reason to fear death—and neither should you be afraid of truly living in every moment of life.

Heaven is not only our future reality; it is also the present reality of every believer. Heaven is real. In fact, once you reach your eternal home with Jesus, you will discover that Heaven is far more real than this earthly experience you now call *reality*.

Our earthly lives are slipping away and quickly fading. That's why Jesus tells us, "Do not store up for yourselves treasures on earth, where moths and vermin destroy, and where thieves break in and steal. But store up for yourselves treasures in heaven" (Matthew 6:19-20). In other words, don't merely invest in your life on earth, but invest in eternity. Invest in Heaven.

I hope this book will serve as your investment guide as you store up eternal treasures in your heavenly home. I want you to be fully prepared because Heaven is *now*, and Heaven is *forever*.

JOY of the HEAVEN

part 1

1

HEAVEN IS ALL ABOUT JESUS

BEFORE FOUNDING The Church of the Apostles, I often traveled overseas on behalf of the Haggai Institute, a leadership training organization for evangelists. Several times a year, I was away from home for two weeks or longer at a time. When I was away, I deeply missed my wife and children. The pain and loneliness of those times of separation were eased only by the knowledge of the joyous reunion that would take place when I returned home.

I knew that, at the end of that long road, I would be greeted with hugs, kisses, and happy faces, and I would catch up on all the events I had missed while I was gone. I think those joyful reunions were but a faint echo of what our reunion in Heaven will be. When I think of Heaven, the image that comes to mind is one of joyful reunions with family members and friends—and above all, the joy of seeing the face of Jesus.

Randy Alcorn beautifully captures the emotions of that reunion in his book titled *Heaven*: "Think of friends or family members who loved Jesus and are with him now. Picture them with you, walking together in this place. All of you have powerful bodies, stronger than those of an Olympic decathlete. You are laughing, playing, talking, and reminiscing. You reach up to a tree to pick an apple or orange. You take a bite. It's so sweet that it's startling. You've never tasted anything so good. Now you see someone coming toward you. It's Jesus, with a big smile on his face. You fall to your knees in worship. He pulls you up and embraces you."[1]

Won't that be amazing? Won't that be thrilling? I can hardly think about Heaven without wanting to leave this earth *right now*. Why would anyone want to cling to this life when Heaven is waiting to receive us?

What Makes Heaven Heavenly?

Let me ask you a question: What is the one thing that makes Heaven heavenly?

Is it the fact that Heaven is made of precious stones and purest gold (Revelation 21:18-21)? Is it the great reunion of believers that will take place there? Is it amazing features such as the tree of life and the river of the water of life? Is it Heaven's immense size and the vast number of mansions it contains?

No, none of these things makes Heaven heavenly. There is really only one aspect that makes Heaven what it is: *the presence of God*. Imagine the joy of seeing God's face, of being physically in the presence of the Lord Jehovah. Think of the blessing of seeing Jesus face-to-face and thanking him for giving his life for your salvation. Next to the privilege of adoring and worshiping him in person, nothing else matters.

Jesus is what makes Heaven heavenly.

All of Heaven's other glorious aspects and features will fill us with wonder and amazement. Certainly we look forward to them. But without Jesus, it would not be Heaven.

To be in Heaven is to behold Jesus face-to-face. To be in Heaven is to behold God the Father face-to-face. In the Psalms, the sons of Korah poetically expressed their deep longing to see God: "As the deer pants for streams of water, so my soul pants for you, my God. My soul thirsts for God, for the living God. When can I go and meet with God?" (Psalm 42:1-2).

The thought of seeing God face-to-face exhilarates me, excites me, and fills me with emotion. It fulfills me and satisfies me completely. The thought of one day meeting God in person ignites my passion and energizes me to work harder for him.

The thought of seeing God face-to-face should comfort us when we grieve and encourage us when we are sick. It should enable us to rejoice amid the disappointments of life. It should empower us to persevere through opposition and adversity.

We will see God! That's what Heaven is all about.

Shekinah Glory

Does the prospect of seeing the face of God thrill you the way it thrills me?

The truth is that not all Christians are thrilled by the idea. Some do not have "seeing the face of God" on their wish list. Others are ambivalent about God or even afraid of him.

As children of God, if we have never contemplated the awe and wonder of seeing his face, we should take some time to think about it. The hope of seeing God face-to-face should be our greatest inspiration. It should be what we live for in this life. It should affect every decision we make. It should motivate us to live and work and speak and sacrifice with the hope of eternity always on our minds.

In the Old Testament, the people of Israel believed that God was present among them in the Holy of Holies, in the Tabernacle or the Temple. They didn't think the Holy of Holies *contained* God, but they believed that he dwelled among his people in a special way, in the form of the shekinah glory—the glory of God that filled the Holy of Holies. (*shekinah* means *dwelling* in Hebrew.)

Though the Old Testament Israelites believed that God dwelled among them in the Holy of Holies, they didn't imagine it could be possible to see God's face. In fact, seeing his face would result in instant death.

Only the high priest was allowed to enter the Holy of Holies, and he went there only once a year. The book of Exodus specifies that the high priest's robes were to be adorned with embroidered pomegranates and small golden bells. "The sound of the bells will be heard," the Lord said, "when he enters the Holy Place before the LORD and when he comes out, so that he will not die" (Exodus 28:35). The bells enabled those outside the Tabernacle to know when the high priest went into and out of the Holy of Holies.

According to an ancient Jewish tradition, the high priest would enter the Holy of Holies on the Day of Atonement, with a gold or scarlet rope tied to his foot. Though Scripture makes no mention of this practice, tradition has it that the purpose of the rope was to make it possible to retrieve the high priest's body if he should ever fail in his duties and be struck dead inside the Holy of Holies. If the golden bells on the high priest's robes went silent, the other priests would know to use the rope to pull the dead man's body out of the Holy of Holies.

No one but the high priest dared to enter the Holy of Holies, because that was where the shekinah glory dwelled, symbolizing the presence of God. Under any other circumstances, for a mere mortal to stand in the presence of God's glory would mean certain death.

There is a fascinating scene in Exodus 33, where Moses says to God, "Show me your glory" (Exodus 33:18).

God replies, "You cannot see my face, for no one may see me and live" (Exodus 33:20). But God, in his mercy, arranged for Moses to stand in a cleft of a rock while he passed by. The hand of God shielded Moses from the glory of God's face. Then God took his hand away, and Moses saw God's back, but not his face (Exodus 33:21-23).

Moses, that great man of God, was not permitted to see the face of God. But you and I will see God's face in Heaven. That is one of the most magnificent promises ever written (Revelation 22:4).

Only Sinless People

"Without holiness," the Bible tells us, "no one will see the Lord" (Hebrews 12:14). At first glance, this seems like bad news for every human being who has ever lived. Who among us is holy? Who among us is undefiled by sin? If only sinless people are permitted to see the face of God, what hope do you and I have? And yet the Bible is clear: "Without holiness no one will see the Lord."

You may be thinking, *You just got through telling me that I will get to see God. And now you're telling me I won't because I'm a sinner! This is the worst news ever!*

Ah, but I'm just getting to the best part.

It's true that you and I are sinners. We have no holiness or righteousness of our own on which to stand before the Lord. But if you have committed your life to Jesus Christ, if he is your Savior and Lord, I *guarantee* you will see God face-to-face.

You will not stand before God clothed in your own filthy rags of "good intentions." Instead, you will stand before him clothed in the radiant white garments of the holiness of Jesus Christ. If you have repented of your sins and received the forgiveness of Jesus, then God the Father will see you through the prism of Jesus, the perfection of Jesus, and the sinlessness of Jesus—and you *will* see the face of God in Heaven.

Without holiness, no one will see the Lord. But Jesus is our holiness. His sinless perfection will be imputed to us. We will stand before God the Father as if we had never sinned at all.

There is a statement I have heard people make many times. I have heard people say it when I have shared the gospel with them. I have heard people say it on talk shows. I have heard people say it in casual conversation. They say something like this: "I believe God is a God of love. When I die, God will accept me. I know I'm not very religious, and I've never paid much attention to Jesus. But I'm not a bad person. If God really is a God of love, he will let me into Heaven."

I can't tell you how many times I've heard people express these sentiments, and I will tell you honestly, I ache inside every time I hear it. It sickens me to know that people are so deceived about God's nature and so careless about their own eternal destiny. Yes, God is a God of love. He loves us so much that he sent his only Son to die in our place so that we can live forever in Heaven. He loves us so much that he offered us salvation as a free gift of grace.

But we must *accept* the gift. We must *repent* of our sins and *receive* the forgiveness that comes only through Jesus. We can't simply drift through life, pursuing our own ambitions and worshiping our own selves, while vaguely assuming that God will grade on a curve and let us into Heaven if we're better than average. God doesn't grade on a curve—it's pass-fail. And the only way to pass is by accepting the holiness and forgiveness of Jesus. Without it, *no one* will see the Lord.

And consider this: If Heaven is all about Jesus, and if you don't love Jesus during your life here on earth, you wouldn't be happy in Heaven anyway. You wouldn't be able to stand it because Heaven is all about Jesus.

We Will See God's Face

Heaven will be a *thrilling* and *fulfilling* eternal experience.

Everyone on earth has unfulfilled hopes and dreams. What are yours? What are your expectations about life that have not been met? What disappointments have you suffered? What promises have people made to you that they haven't kept? What opportunities in life have you missed that will never come your way again?

In Heaven, all of your longings will be satisfied forever. Why? Because you will be in the presence of God, seeing him face-to-face, and that will be the fulfillment of all the longings of your earthly life. When you finally behold God in all his glory, you will know complete satisfaction and joy for the first time ever.

In the Sermon on the Mount, Jesus gives us a beautiful promise: "Blessed are the pure in heart, for they will see God" (Matthew 5:8). The Greek word for *pure* in this verse is *katharos*, which means blameless and unstained by guilt. Who are the pure in heart? Those who have been made blameless, whose guilty, sinful stains have been washed away by the blood of Jesus.

What lies ahead for the pure in heart? They will see God in Heaven.

These words of Jesus remind us of the promise in Revelation 22:3-4: "The throne of God and of the Lamb [Jesus] will be in the city [the New Jerusalem], and his servants will serve him. They will see his face, and his name will be on their foreheads." Who are the servants of Jesus? The pure in heart, the ones who will see God's face.

How Can We See the Invisible God?

At this point, you may be thinking, *How are we going to see God's face? Doesn't the Bible teach that God is a spirit?* These are important questions.

It's true that God is a spirit. As Jesus told the woman at the well in Samaria, "God is spirit, and his worshipers must worship in the Spirit and in truth" (John 4:24). Jesus, the Son of God, came to earth in human flesh and lived among us, but God the Father did not. Jesus has a human body, but God the Father is spirit.

The Bible sometimes speaks of God as if he has a human body. For example, when Moses hid in the cleft of the rock on Mount Sinai, he was allowed to see God's "back" but not his "face." It's not easy for us to understand what that meant in Moses' experience. But we know that God must have passed by in some glorious manifestation and that Moses saw the glory, but he was not permitted to see God's face.

We know that, elsewhere in Scripture, God is described in anthropomorphic terms—that is, using words that figuratively attribute physical, humanlike characteristics to God so that we can understand and relate to him. In Isaiah 59:1, the prophet says, "Surely the arm of the LORD is not too short to save, nor his ear too dull to hear." And 2 Chronicles 16:9 says, "For the eyes of the LORD range throughout the earth." It's important to understand that this is metaphorical language, not to be taken literally.

The clearly literal passages of Scripture that tell us about God's true nature always describe him as *spirit*. After Solomon completed the construction of the great Temple in Jerusalem, he acknowledged that God, as a spirit, could not be contained within a house made of stone: "Will God really dwell on earth with humans? The heavens, even the highest heavens, cannot contain you. How much less this temple I have built!" (2 Chronicles 6:18).

The apostle Paul tells us that God, being a spirit, is invisible: "The Son is the image of the invisible God, the firstborn over all creation" (Colossians 1:15). Paul also wrote, "Now to the King eternal, immortal, invisible, the only God, be honor and glory for ever and ever. Amen" (1 Timothy 1:17).

So, since God is an invisible spirit, how will we see his face in Heaven?

Seeing with Resurrection Eyes

We must never forget that we will have new, spiritual, resurrection bodies in Heaven. They will be like the resurrection body of Jesus. Remember how, a week after the Resurrection, Jesus appeared to Thomas and the other disciples? John 20:26 tells us, "Though the doors were locked, Jesus came and stood among them and said, 'Peace be with you!'" Locked doors were no barrier to Jesus—yet his resurrection body was visible and physical as well as spiritual. Jesus invited Thomas to touch the wounds he had suffered on the cross.

Our resurrection bodies will presumably be like Christ's, perfect and unlimited by physical infirmities or barriers. We will be recognizable, but completed and perfected. We will have all the supernatural, spiritual knowledge that we sadly lack in this earthly life. Our earthly eyes are fallen eyes, diseased and clouded by the effects of sin. But our resurrection eyes will see all that is invisible to our earthly, mortal eyes. Our resurrection eyes will see the face of God.

We can't imagine what the face of God the Father will look like to our resurrection eyes. But we know that we will see what Moses was never allowed to see in his earthly body. We will see the ultimate reality of God's face.

And yes, we are also going to see the face of Jesus. We will see him in all his resurrected glory, in his perfect resurrected body, with all his resurrected power. We will see him as John saw him in the vision of Revelation—"dressed in a robe reaching down to his feet and with a golden sash around his chest. The hair on his head was white like wool, as white as snow, and his eyes were like blazing fire. . . . His face was like the sun shining in all its brilliance" (Revelation 1:13-16).

I've heard some people claim that the Old Testament

Israelites had no concept of Heaven and no belief in the afterlife. That claim ignores numerous Old Testament passages that speak of Heaven or the afterlife. (See, for example, Genesis 5:24; 1 Kings 22:19; 2 Kings 2:9-12; Psalm 16:10, 49:15, 73:24-26; Isaiah 6:1, 25:8, 26:19; and Daniel 12:1-3.)

The most explicit expression in the Old Testament of the hope of a physical resurrection is that of Job, who fully expected to see the face of God in Heaven: "I know that my redeemer lives, and that in the end he will stand on the earth. And after my skin has been destroyed, yet in my flesh I will see God" (Job 19:25-26).

Job said he would see God in Heaven. Jesus said that the pure in heart will see God in Heaven. Revelation says we will see God's face in Heaven. From the Old Testament to the New, Scripture consistently promises that we will see God face-to-face in Heaven. Can there be any greater hope and assurance than that?

The expectation that we will see God's face in our resurrection bodies is both thrilling and fulfilling beyond our comprehension. We can't imagine it now, but when the moment comes, we will experience Heaven to the fullest, highest, deepest, widest, most meaningful extent.

The End of All Deceptions and Delusions
Whenever you consider one of God's magnificent creations—mountains, oceans, stars and planets, the magnificent intricacies of the human body—remind yourself that these are mere glimpses and foretastes of the glories we will see in Heaven.

Everything in Heaven will be unimaginably more magnificent than any of the wonders of earth and the universe.

The face of God will be the greatest wonder of all.

Heaven will be the ultimate experience because there will be no deceptions or delusions there. There will be no sin to separate us from God or from one another. In Heaven we will see God as he is, and we will see ourselves and one another as God sees us.

How does God see us? He sees us as a cherished work of his creation. He sees us as his workmanship, precious in his sight.

How do we see each other? We may think we see other people as God's workmanship—and in our most charitable and godly moments, perhaps we do. But the real test of how we view others comes when we are driving and someone cuts in front of us and we have to slam on the brakes to avoid an accident. The words that come out of our mouths at that moment will tell us how we really see other people. Do we bless and forgive them as God's precious creations—or do we curse or revile them?

In Heaven, we will see each other as God sees us. All anger and hatred, all suspicion and defensiveness, all temptation and sin will be no more. All disappointments will become divine appointments. All discontentment will be replaced with eternal contentment.

The Restoration of God's Tangible Presence

Theologians often speak of Heaven as the restoration of the lost Garden of Eden. And that is true in many ways. For example, the tree of life, which was taken from the earth when Eden was lost, will be replanted in the new Jerusalem. The splendor and beauty of Eden will be everywhere throughout Heaven. All of that is true.

But I think many people misunderstand the true source of Eden's splendor and beauty. It wasn't the trees and flowering plants, the abundant food that grew everywhere, the waterfalls and streams, or the many varieties of peaceful animals that made Eden what it was. Though all those things were amazing and wonderful, of course, none of them were the source of Eden's magnificence and glory.

No, Eden was astonishingly beautiful *because God was present there.* Genesis 3:8 tells us, "The man and his wife heard the sound of the LORD God as he was walking in the garden in the cool of the day." I don't know how figurative this statement is, but it certainly sounds quite literal. There is some sense in which God, taking humanlike form, was present in the Garden of Eden. Before sin entered the world, Adam and Eve were accustomed to seeing God face-to-face in the Garden. They had fellowship with him. They talked to him.

But after the Fall they hid from him.

Humanity would not have a direct experience with God again until the shekinah glory of God came from Heaven in the person of Jesus Christ and dwelt among us for a time.

Today, we have a glimpse of what it is like to experience the presence of God because the Holy Spirit dwells in us. The Spirit guides us and comforts us and fills us with joy.

But because of our fallen, un-resurrected state, our experience of God's presence is limited and incomplete. In Heaven, we will experience God in a way that is limitless, complete, and beyond our present comprehension. Once again, human beings will be able to walk with God in the cool of the day in the gardens of Heaven. We will see him face-to-face.

When we arrive in Heaven and see the face of Jesus, all of the puzzlements of this life will be solved. All our present painful experiences will be transformed into heavenly delights. Our tears will become oceans of joy. Our pain will become clouds of endless beauty.

Your Ticket to Heaven

Here's the most important question of all: If you were to die today, are you sure you would be in Heaven?

Someone once asked me, "How can you be certain you are going to Heaven?" Before I could reply, the person continued, "That seems like an arrogant, presumptuous statement. The closest I can come is to say, 'I *hope* I'll go to Heaven,' but I really can't be sure. I think it's a sign of humility to say, 'I hope so,' and leave it at that."

I said, "My beloved friend, the certainty of Heaven that you mistake for arrogance in me is what sets the Christian faith apart from all other religions. God himself promised that, if we surrender to Jesus Christ in repentance and faith, our salvation is assured. We don't have to 'hope' we'll go to Heaven. It's not a matter of 'maybe' or 'possibly.' God has given us a rock-solid assurance that we will see him in Heaven."

When you receive Jesus Christ into your life and begin your walk with him, you will discover that this life is but a train ride—and every one of us will get off at a station along the way. Your journey may end in thirty minutes, thirty days, thirty years, but the train ride will eventually, and inevitably, come to an end.

But if you are walking with Jesus, your train ride will end at a station called Heaven. That is your destination. Your train ticket is stamped for "Heaven," and that is where you'll get off the train and live throughout eternity.

And here's more good news: When you walk with Jesus, eternity in Heaven doesn't begin when you die. It begins when you say "yes" to Jesus. Eternal life begins at that moment, and it never ends. When you step off that train in Heaven and see the face of God, you will experience unspeakable joy.

The right to stand before God, robed in the righteousness and sinlessness of Jesus, has been purchased in your name by the blood of Jesus Christ. When he died on the cross, he purchased all the tickets that will get you and me and every other believer into Heaven. He has those tickets in his nail-scarred hands.

The blood of Jesus is your ticket to Heaven. Apart from the blood of Jesus, you can never enter Heaven and you can never see the face of God.

And here is something else that is vital to understand: Satan is printing up phony tickets. He is handing out these counterfeits to millions of people and deceiving them into thinking they have free passage to Heaven. Satan's phony tickets say nothing about the blood of Jesus. Instead, they say you can enter Heaven through your good works, good intentions, or good vibes; or through the teachings of Muhammad, the Dalai Lama, L. Ron Hubbard, Joseph Smith, Mary Baker Eddy, or a New Age guru. All these "alternate paths" are phony tickets to Heaven, printed up by Satan.

How do you know if you have a genuine ticket to Heaven? That's easy: It's only genuine if it was paid for by the blood of Jesus.

Eternal Life in View

One Sunday morning, evangelist Charles E. Fuller announced on his radio program, *The Old Fashioned Revival Hour*, that his next week's sermon would be about Heaven. During the week, he received a letter from a man who was in the final stages of a terminal illness.

The letter read in part, "Next Sunday you are to talk about Heaven. I am interested in that land, because I have held a clear title to a bit of property there for over fifty-five years. I did not buy it. It was given to me without money and without price. But the donor purchased it for me at tremendous sacrifice. . . . Termites can never undermine its foundations for they rest on the rock of ages. Fire cannot destroy it. Floods cannot wash it away."[2]

These are the words of a man who was living the last days of his earthly life with eternity in view. Eagerly anticipating leaving this world behind, with all of its sorrows, he looked forward to moving into his eternal home and seeing the face of God.

All believers will arrive at their eternal destination, a place called Heaven. But not all believers will receive the same rewards in eternity. Paul writes, "We make it our goal to please him, whether we are at home in the body or away from it. For we must all appear before the judgment seat of Christ, so that each of us may receive what is due us for the things done while in the body, whether good or bad" (2 Corinthians 5:9-10).

Jesus has already resolved our eternal destiny. It was settled when he died on the cross and said, "It is finished," and it was settled when we repented of our sins and received the forgiveness and eternal life he freely offers us. But Jesus will judge us in eternity—not for our sins, but for the works we have done in this life. He will reward us for the works we do in faith and obedience.

In his parable of the talents, Jesus talks about the judgment and rewarding of his followers. Those who serve him faithfully will hear the voice of the master, Jesus, saying, "Well done, good and faithful servant! You have been faithful with a few things; I will put you in charge of many things. Come and share your master's happiness!" (Matthew 25:23).

If you have placed your trust in Jesus Christ, you are going to live in Heaven, with Jesus, forever. If you are wise and faithful, you will spend the remainder of this life preparing for the next. You will serve Jesus faithfully, looking forward to the day when you see God face-to-face and we hear Jesus say, "Well done, good and faithful servant!"

2

THE BEAUTY OF HEAVEN

AN AUTHOR WHOSE NAME I can't recall recently appeared on a show to promote his book and discuss his views on life and meaning. The author was an atheist. He didn't believe in life after death, and he talked about how the ancient Greek Stoics didn't believe in life after death either. Instead, they tried to live a satisfying life in the moment.

The interviewer asked, "Do you ever think about your own mortality?"

The author, who was in his sixties, replied, "I try not to think about death. I'm older now, and my death is much closer than it used to be. Somewhere in my thirties or forties, I discovered that my time horizon flipped. In my younger years, I was living from my birth. Now that I'm older, I'm living toward my death. So I try not to dwell on my mortality."

Maybe you identify with those words. There may have been a time in your life, possibly in your thirties or forties, when you realized your "time horizon" had changed. It gradually dawned on you that you were no longer looking backward to your childhood and the family you were raised in. Instead, you realized you are living toward your death.

When you are living toward your death, you start asking questions such as, "When I die, what will my life have meant? What have I been living for? Have I spent my limited allotment of years on what truly matters? How will God judge my life?"

Thank God, we don't have to live as the Stoics lived, lacking any hope for the afterlife. And we don't have to live as that atheist author lived, avoiding the subject of our own mortality and the swift approach of death.

As believers and followers of Jesus Christ, we are assured of eternity in Heaven. We are free to think about and dwell on our own mortality because we know that death is not the end of the story. A beautiful home awaits us in Heaven.

Let's take some time together now to dwell on the majesty, glory, and beauty that awaits us in our eternal home.

Eight Beautiful Facets of Heaven

A facet is a geometrically arranged flat surface on a gemstone that reflects the light and reveals the inner beauty of the stone. Faceted gemstones, such as cut diamonds, rubies, and emeralds, are stones of exquisite color, sparkle, and beauty.

I think of Heaven as very much like a faceted gemstone. In fact, the description of Heaven in Revelation 21 describes the foundations of the heavenly city in terms of precious stones— sapphire, agate, emerald, onyx, ruby, and more. John describes Heaven as having a wall made of jasper (a cryptocrystalline quartz found in a variety of colors) and city structures made of pure gold, "as pure as glass" (Revelation 21:18).

These are beautiful images, and they all suggest that Heaven is a place of color, sparkle, and beauty, like a brilliantly faceted gemstone. Yet these striking physical descriptions of Heaven don't excite me nearly as much as the deeper realities of Heaven—realities that I call *the eight beautiful facets of Heaven*. Let's take a close look at each one.

Facet #1: Uninterrupted Fellowship

Every other facet of Heaven pales in comparison to this one: We will look upon the face of Jesus. We will be in his presence continually. We will have unending, unbroken fellowship with him throughout eternity. We will be in the everlasting presence of the one who loves us and saved us through his death on the cross.

In 1 Corinthians 13:12, Paul tells us that "now we see only a reflection as in a mirror; then we shall see face to face. Now I know in part; then I shall know fully, even as I am fully known." In Paul's day, you couldn't buy the kind of mirrors we have today—a sheet of glass with a coating of silver on the back to provide a perfect and clear reflection. In those days, mirrors were made out of polished metal or a very imperfect and impure glass. The reflection they provided was not very clear or bright. So, Paul spoke of this present life as seeing a reflection in a mirror—or as the King James Version renders his words, "We see through a glass, darkly."

But in Heaven, Paul proclaims, "we shall see face to face." We shall see Jesus face-to-face. We shall see God the Father face-to-face. We shall see reality—transcendent, eternal reality—as it truly is. There will be no barriers or limits to our understanding.

"Someone once asked a Christian what he expected to do when he got to heaven," writes Dwight L. Moody in his book titled *Heaven*. "He said he expected to spend the first thousand years looking at Jesus Christ, and after that he would look for Peter, and then for James, and for John. . . . But it seems to me that one look at Jesus Christ will more than reward us for all we have ever done for Him down here, for all the sacrifices we can possibly make for Him, just to see Him; only to see Him."[1]

What makes Heaven heavenly is that Jesus lives there. If Jesus were not there, it would not be Heaven. Praise God, Jesus is in Heaven, preparing a place for us—our eternal home where we will enjoy uninterrupted fellowship with him.

We will also experience uninterrupted fellowship with all our loved ones who have died in the Lord. Later in this book, we will look at what the Bible calls the New Heaven and the New Earth. But for now I want to talk about the present

Heaven (or Paradise), where Christians go the moment they die. When we say that a loved one "has gone to Heaven," we are referring to Paradise, the present Heaven.

It is important that we distinguish between the present Heaven—where our saved and deceased loved ones are right now as we all await the return of Jesus Christ and the resurrection of the dead—and the future New Heaven, where we are destined to live forever in the presence of Jesus. All the great promises of redemption will be fulfilled in the New Heaven, where we will live forever in our resurrection bodies. In the meantime, we look forward to the joys and glories of the present Heaven.

The present Heaven is a beautiful and awe-inspiring place, which is why Jesus, Paul, and John call it Paradise (Luke 23:43; 2 Corinthians 12:4; Revelation 2:7). This is the Heaven Ezekiel saw when he said, "The heavens were opened and I saw visions of God" (Ezekiel 1:1). This is the Heaven the martyr Stephen saw moments before his death, when he said, "I see heaven open and the Son of Man standing at the right hand of God" (Acts 7:56). This is the Heaven that Paul visited, where he "heard inexpressible things, things that no one is permitted to tell" (2 Corinthians 12:4).

Please don't fall for the unfounded, unbiblical claim that your loved ones are in an unconscious state of "soul sleep." That's a false doctrine. You won't find it anywhere in the Bible. (When the Bible speaks of those who have "fallen asleep," it is merely using a metaphor for physical death.) Throughout Scripture, we consistently find descriptions of the present Heaven as a wonderful place where there is communion, fellowship, consciousness, and joy. All those who have died in Jesus are enjoying the blessings of the present Heaven. Because being in the present Heaven means being with Jesus, it is "better by far" than being on earth (Philippians 1:23).

Until the New Heaven appears, the present Heaven will be a place of reunions, communion, and rejoicing. There will be laughter and singing—and it will all take place in the presence of our Lord Jesus. The moment our eyes close in death, we will awaken to a heavenly welcome, fully conscious, fully aware, in a place Jesus calls *Paradise.* Our loved ones in the faith are there now, experiencing vibrant relationships with Jesus and with one another as they await the resurrection and the arrival of the New Heaven and New Earth.

Facet #2: Rest from Spiritual Battles

In Revelation 14:13, John writes, "Then I heard a voice from heaven say, 'Write this: Blessed are the dead who die in the Lord from now on.' 'Yes,' says the Spirit, 'they will rest from their labor, for their deeds will follow them.'"

Resting from our labor doesn't mean we will be idle in Heaven. Many people seem to have a mental image of Heaven derived from medieval paintings of chubby baby angels on clouds strumming harps. I don't know where the artists got their ideas, but this imagery led to a false view of Heaven as a place where everyone becomes an angel. This is a fallacy and has nothing to do with the reality of Heaven.

We will not just be sitting around in Heaven—but we will have rest from Satan's constant opposition and oppression and temptation. We will have rest from the spiritual battles of this life. There will be no more temptation, no more attacks, no more satanic persecution.

Just as the Sabbath was set apart, so eternity is set apart. God established the Sabbath not as a golf day or a day at the beach, but as a day for taking our minds off our everyday plans and labors so that we can focus on God. It is the Sabbath unto the Lord. As Jesus said to the Pharisees, "The Sabbath was made for man, not man for the Sabbath" (Mark 2:27).

God made the Sabbath for human beings because he knew how forgetful we are. He knew that we tend to get busy, and then we leave God out of our thinking. So God made the Sabbath as a time when we could focus on him for one entire day. We are to focus on his holiness, his majesty, his dominion, his power, his mercy, his love, his forgiveness, his grace. He should be our sole focus.

In Heaven, when we have our eternal rest, we will have an everlasting Sabbath, where we can spend all of our time—free from earthly labors, earthly cares, and earthly temptations—focusing on God. It will be a more exciting and intense experience than any theme park thrill ride or any pulse-pounding movie because we will commune face-to-face with the Creator of the universe. As the Sabbath is holy unto the Lord, so too all of eternity will be holy unto the Lord. It will be a restful yet thrilling experience of communion with God.

Have you ever wondered why we live in a universe surrounded by billions and billions of galaxies and stars? Have you wondered why the universe is so vast (according to astronomers) that it would take a beam of light 93 billion years to travel from one end of the observable universe to the other?[2] Well, how would you like to explore the whole universe without any physical limitation? In the New Heaven and the New Earth, the God of infinite power will be with us at all times, personally revealing his wonders to us as we continually give him our praise, thanks, and worship.

Facet #3: Serving Jesus

How do we know we will not be idle in Heaven? Because Revelation 22:3 tells us: "The throne of God and of the Lamb will be in the city, and his servants will serve him." In Heaven, all believers will have the honor and privilege of serving Jesus full time, throughout eternity.

In our transformed resurrection bodies, we will devote our endless energy to serving the living God. We will spend our mental capacities comprehending the love of God. In the New Heaven and the New Earth, we will serve him in ways we can't even imagine now. We will be busy in Heaven, serving God—not grudgingly as we so often do now, but joyfully and enthusiastically.

Whatever work God gives us to do in Heaven will not be a chore or a burden. We will not become fatigued in service to our God. Instead, we will serve God gladly out of gratitude because he has redeemed us. As we serve God in Heaven, we will experience the ultimate fulfillment that has eluded us so often in life.

The Bible gives us an indication of what kind of service it will be: We will reign and rule with God. Have you ever thought about what it will mean to rule with God? Paul writes, "If we endure, we will also reign with him" (2 Timothy 2:12). And John observes that the resurrected believers "will be priests of God and of Christ and will reign with him for a thousand years" (Revelation 20:6).

Jesus, in his parable of the servants, tells us that those who serve faithfully will hear the master say, "Well done, good and faithful servant! You have been faithful with a few things; I will put you in charge of many things. Come and share your master's happiness!" (Matthew 25:23). Will you get to hear those words in Heaven? If you live your earthly life in faithfulness to the Master, he will give you even greater work to do in eternity.

Facet #4: Full Knowledge
In this life, we are filled with questions: Why do the innocent suffer? Why do the wicked prosper? Why do children sometimes come down with incurable diseases? Why do earthquakes and hurricanes devastate the land and kill many people? Now we have only questions. But in Heaven, we will have full knowledge and complete understanding of all these mysteries. As Paul writes in 1 Corinthians 13:12, "Now I know in part; then I shall know fully, even as I am fully known."

In Heaven, we will see all things clearly because we will see them from God's perspective. There will be no need to ask questions. We will understand justice from God's vantage point, and we will be satisfied. We will understand free will and God's sovereign election from his point of view, and we will be satisfied. We will be able to think God's thoughts after him because we will finally have his view of reality. No one in Heaven or in Hell will be able to say, "God, you have been unfair. God, you have misjudged this situation." We will have full knowledge in Heaven.

Facet #5: Righteousness and Purity

We will live holy, righteous, and pure lives in Heaven. God will replace our sinful, fallen hearts with pure hearts that want to live in holiness and purity. Anyone who showed up in Heaven without being transformed by God would be miserable there. As Cardinal John Henry Newman explains, "If we wished to imagine a punishment for an unholy, reprobate soul, we perhaps could not fancy a greater [punishment] than to *summon it to heaven*. Heaven would be hell to an irreligious man."[3]

Think about it. The unregenerate mind and unregenerate heart, with all their sin and rebellion, could not stand the beauty and purity of Heaven. An atmosphere of purity and righteousness would be sickening to the person who hasn't been born again. Heaven would be totally alien to such a person. As Revelation 21:27 tells us, "Nothing impure will ever enter it, nor will anyone who does what is shameful or deceitful, but only those whose names are written in the Lamb's book of life."

How can you know that your name is written in the Lamb's Book of Life? Jesus is the Lamb, the crucified sacrifice for our sins. To have your name written in the Book of Life, you must accept his sacrifice on the cross as the payment for your sins. In other words (as we saw in chapter 1), you must be born again. You must admit that you are a sinner and you must commit your life to Jesus Christ as your Lord and Savior.

If you have received Jesus as your Lord and Savior, if you have longed for righteousness, if you have longed for purity, if you have longed for holiness, then your name is written in the Lamb's Book of Life. But those who have rejected the Lord Jesus, his salvation, his moral demands, and his gift of eternal life have no part in Jesus, in his Kingdom, or in Heaven. Their names are not recorded in the Book of Life.

Having your name recorded in the Book of Life is not the same thing as having your name on a church membership roll. There are many people who have been church members for decades whose names are not written in the Book of Life. They attend church, but they don't have Jesus living in them and through them. They have never been born again. However, the moment someone chooses to follow the Lord Jesus Christ and surrender to him as Savior and Lord, his or her name is written in the Book of Life—not in pencil, not in ink, but in the priceless and indelible blood of Jesus.

Facet #6: Abundance of Life

The Bible promises that, in Heaven, we will live in abundance: "To the thirsty I will give water without cost from the spring of the water of life" (Revelation 21:6). Revelation 22:1-2 describes "the river of the water of life, as clear as crystal, flowing from the throne of God and of the Lamb down the middle of the great street of the city. On each side of the river stood the tree of life, bearing twelve crops of fruit, yielding its fruit every month. And the leaves of the tree are for the healing of the nations."

Heaven is a place of unimaginable plenty. It is a city without hunger because there is an abundance of every kind of fruit. It is a city without cemeteries, for there is no death there. It is a city without hospitals because there is no pain or sickness. It is a city without mental health services because there is no sorrow or stress or despair.

The first two chapters of Genesis show us what God intended for the human beings he created. God created Eden and placed the man and the woman in a garden of abundance. And God's plan for Heaven is to create a new Eden in the form of the New Heaven and New Earth. The last two chapters of Revelation mirror the first two chapters of Genesis, because we see God restoring his creation to an even better and more abundant state than the original Eden.

Genesis 1 and 2 show us God's act of creation. Revelation 21 and 22 show us God's act of re-creation and restoration. And in both the Genesis and Revelation passages, we see that God lavishes an abundance of blessing on his people.

Facet #7: Continuous Glory

Many (if not most) Christians draw a blank when they hear the word *glory*. It doesn't seem to have much meaning to modern minds. So when people come across the word *glory* in the Bible, they either shrug it off as a mystery or they misinterpret and misunderstand what the word means. What does the Bible mean by *glory*?

In the Bible, *glory* refers to the revelation of the character of God in Jesus Christ. In his prayer before going to the cross, Jesus prayed, "Father, the hour has come. Glorify your Son, that your Son may glorify you" (John 17:1). In other words, Jesus prayed that the glorious reality of God the Father would shine through him from the cross. When we are in Heaven, we will be transformed so that the glorious reality of God's character will be revealed in us and through us.

As you read through the letters of the apostle Paul, you see that he frequently talks about Heaven. Paul sets an example for you and me. I am convinced that there is something wrong with our faith if we do not spend a great deal of time looking to Heaven and thinking about Heaven.

Paul was constantly preaching the gospel, planting churches, and debating with Jewish religious leaders or Greek philosophers. He tirelessly worked to win souls and expand the Kingdom of God. As he served the Lord Jesus, he endured suffering. He was flogged nearly to death five times. Three times he was beaten with rods. He was shipwrecked three times. Once he was stoned and left for dead. As he traveled, he risked being robbed or killed by bandits. He was persecuted by the Romans, by the Jewish religious leaders, and even by false Christians who spread lies about him in the church (2 Corinthians 11:24-26).

Yet, despite all the hardship he faced, Paul was able to say, "For our light and momentary troubles are achieving for us an eternal glory that far outweighs them all" (2 Corinthians 4:17). Paul didn't focus on his sufferings; he focused on Heaven. And compared with the glory of Heaven, all of his sufferings seemed "light and momentary." What was true for Paul is true for you and me as well. All of life's afflictions—no matter how painful and burdensome they seem to us now—will one day seem as light as a feather when weighed against the blessings and glory of Heaven.

When we get to Heaven, we will experience the glory of God, the character of God, and the presence of God. The righteousness of God will shine through us as we live in our resurrection bodies. That is why Paul writes, "When Christ, who is your life, appears, then you also will appear with him in glory" (Colossians 3:4). Everything that God is, everything that God has, he will share with us—including his glory.

Facet #8: Constant Worship

The idea of continuous, nonstop worship may not sound appealing to you now. In fact, some people have actually said they are *afraid* of going to Heaven because it's going to be like sitting in church, singing hymns forever and ever. One prominent British politician said that, before he became a born-again Christian, he feared Heaven would be like an endless, boring eleven o'clock church service—and that, in his mind, would be like Hell.

But Heaven is not going to be at all like an earthly church service. Yes, we will be praising and thanking Jesus. Yes, we will experience the most wonderful music ever composed. But true worship is so much more than praise and singing.

The word *worship* comes from an Old English word describing the state of being *worthy* or *honorable*. We worship God because he alone is worthy of our praise and thankfulness. True heavenly worship is not a weekly ritual like attending church—it's an all-consuming way of life. It is gratefully enjoying God's presence. It is the unimaginable joy of seeing our Lord face-to-face. I don't know about you, but I'm ready—and I can't wait to get there.

If you are of a certain generation, you are familiar with the music of singer-songwriter David Crosby. Not long before he died on January 18, 2023, Crosby responded on his Twitter account to another user's tweet about Heaven: "I heard the place is overrated . . . cloudy."[4] Whether his response was merely tongue in cheek or indicative of his true feelings, I don't know, but my heart breaks for anyone who would think so little of Heaven—and of their own eternal destiny. Heaven is not overrated. We can't begin to imagine the excitement and unspeakable joy we will experience as we worship the Lord there. John described the ecstatic jubilation in Heaven with these words: "I heard what sounded like the roar of a great multitude in heaven shouting: 'Hallelujah! Salvation and glory and power belong to our God'" (Revelation 19:1).

Our praises to God in Heaven will be centered around the worthiness of the Lord Jesus Christ. On that day, a vast crowd of saints will be gathered, including Abraham, Moses, Joshua, Elijah, David, Peter, John, James, and Paul—and you and I will be there, all worshiping the Lord Jesus Christ together.

I can almost hear the shouts of "Hallelujah!" and the crescendo of the heavenly choir. There will be Jewish believers and Gentile believers, Black believers and White believers, Democrat believers and Republican believers, Pakistani believers and Indian believers, Russian believers and Ukrainian believers, Chinese and Japanese and Korean believers. They will all be united in worshiping the Lord Jesus Christ.

John also records, "After this I looked, and there before me was a great multitude that no one could count, from every nation, tribe, people and language, standing before the throne and before the Lamb. They were wearing white robes and were holding palm branches in their hands. And they cried out in a loud voice: 'Salvation belongs to our God, who sits on the throne, and to the Lamb'" (Revelation 7:9-10).

Note the phrase "they cried out in a loud voice." The worship of the Lord will be thunderous in Heaven. What a day that will be!

Escorted by Angels

In Jesus' account of Lazarus and the rich man in Luke 16, and we find evidence that this story is not a parable, but rather the Lord's true account of two men who lived and died and went on to the afterlife. (We discuss this story in greater detail in chapter 9.) And there is one detail in the story that often goes unnoticed. In verse 22, Jesus says, "The time came when the beggar died and the angels carried him to Abraham's side. The rich man also died and was buried."

Lazarus the beggar was *carried by angels* to Abraham's side. But there were no angels attending the death of the rich man. When he died, he simply was buried.

When a believer dies, guardian angels escort that believer to Heaven. When you close your eyes in death, your angel is there with you. I believe that your angel stays in Heaven with you—because, after all, the angel needs to teach you how to worship! Most of us don't know how to worship, but we will have angels to instruct us.

In Revelation 22, John describes how an angel showed him all the wonders and glories of Heaven. John was so astounded and moved by all that he saw that he could not stand: "I fell down to worship at the feet of the angel who had been showing [these things] to me."

But the angel refused to accept John's worship. "Don't do that!" the angel said. "I am a fellow servant with you and with your fellow prophets and with all who keep the words of this scroll. Worship God!" (Revelation 22:8-9).

John had to learn that the worship of angels is idolatry. The only one worthy of worship is the triune God—one God in three persons. But even though we must never worship angels or any other created thing, we can be excited to

know that angels will be in Heaven and we can meet them
and learn from them.

The True Focus of Life

In a cemetery in Philadelphia, there is an epitaph that the
great American founding father Benjamin Franklin wrote for
himself:

> The Body of
> B. Franklin, Printer,
> Like the Cover of an old Book,
> Its Contents torn out,
> And Stript of its Lettering & Gilding,
> Lies here, Food for Worms.
> But the Work shall not be lost,
> For it will as he believ'd
> appear once more
> In a new and more elegant Edition
> Corrected and improved
> By the Author.[5]

The "Author" Franklin refers to, of course, is God.
Franklin had a proper understanding of life and eternity. His
hope was in the Lord—and he looked forward to eternity in
his "corrected and improved" resurrection body in Heaven.

Our lives should be focused on a single reality: *where we
will spend eternity*. When you buy a house, you inspect it.
Why? Because you plan to spend years living in that house.

So doesn't it make good sense to think seriously about where you will spend all of eternity?

Atheists often accuse Christians of being "escapists" because of our belief in Heaven. And I would reply that, yes, I'm an escapist. I want to escape from this life and all of its sin and sorrow and death. I want to escape the horrors of the Great Tribulation that are coming upon the world. I want to escape the terrors and torments of Hell and damnation.

So, thank you, Jesus, for providing a way of escape through your death on the cross. And thank you, Jesus, for going to Heaven to prepare a place for me. And thank you, Jesus, for providing a place where, when this earthly life is over, I can escape to the welcoming arms of my Savior and Master.

Escape to Heaven! What a wonderful experience to anticipate.

In the opening chapter of Acts, Jesus is taken up into the clouds and an angel tells his followers, "This same Jesus, who has been taken from you into heaven, will come back in the same way you have seen him go into heaven" (Acts 1:11). Thank God, Jesus did not ascend to an abstract idea, or to a metaphor, or to wishful thinking. Jesus went to a *literal place* called Heaven.

In Heaven, we will have real resurrection bodies—just like the resurrection body of Jesus. We will live in a real eternal home.

One day, my earthly body will die and be buried—but no one can bury my eternal life. All the gravediggers in the world cannot make a hole wide enough, long enough, or deep enough to swallow up my eternal life. Eternal life is mine because Jesus says so, because he died so I can be born again.

D. L. Moody quoted a humble woman who said that the way to Heaven is "short, easy, and simple . . . out of self, into Christ, and into glory."[6] You can't make it any plainer than that. Let's not overcomplicate what it means to go to Heaven. Let's trust in Jesus, because he has prepared a beautiful place for you and me to spend all of eternity.

3

THE BENEFITS OF HEAVEN

In 1984, I became a citizen of the United States, after emigrating from Egypt to America in the mid-1970s. I relinquished my citizenship in the country of my birth and became a citizen of this freedom-loving nation. I love the United States and I feel privileged to live here.

But as much as I love America, it does not hold the attraction for me that Heaven does. Though I am happy to be a US citizen, my ultimate citizenship is in Heaven. I became a naturalized citizen of Heaven when I placed my trust in Jesus Christ and became a partaker of his divine nature.

Paul also reminds us that we don't belong here on earth. This planet is not our home. He urges us to be continually aware that "our citizenship is in heaven. And we eagerly await a Savior from there, the Lord Jesus Christ" (Philippians 3:20).

In the Sermon on the Mount, Jesus reminds us, "Do not store up for yourselves treasures on earth, where moths and vermin destroy, and where thieves break in and steal. But store up for yourselves treasures in heaven, where moths and vermin do not destroy, and where thieves do not break in and steal" (Matthew 6:19-20).

The Ten Benefits of Heaven

As born-again believers in the Lord Jesus Christ, we have treasures stored up in Heaven. Paul, in Ephesians 2:7, calls these treasures "the incomparable riches of his grace." I call them the Ten Benefits of Heaven. Let's look at each of these ten benefits that are kept in Heaven for us because we have received Jesus as the Lord and Savior of our lives.

Benefit #1: Resurrection from Sin and Death

Paul opens Ephesians 2 with this statement: "You were dead in your transgressions and sins, in which you used to live when you followed the ways of this world and of the ruler of the kingdom of the air, the spirit who is now at work in those who are disobedient. . . . [But] God, who is rich in mercy, made us alive with Christ" (Ephesians 2:1-2, 4-5).

God, through Jesus Christ, has resurrected us from sin and from death. This foundational Christian truth is diametrically opposed to the biggest and worst lie ever spread—namely, that if you are *a good person*, you will go to Heaven.

In traveling across the globe and studying the great religions of the world, I have found that this great lie permeates *all* religions. It is the modern equivalent of Satan deceiving Adam and Eve in the Garden of Eden. *But it is antithetical to the Christian faith.*

Here's the truth, straight from God's Word: There is only *one* good person in Heaven, and that's Jesus. Everyone else in Heaven is *a bad person saved by grace.* If you rely on being a "good person" to get to Heaven, you are going to Hell. Only bad people go to Heaven. As Paul writes in Romans 3:12, "All have turned away, they have together become worthless; there is no one who does good, not even one."

In writing to the church at Ephesus, Paul also said, "You were dead in your transgressions and sins" (Ephesians 2:1). Not sick, not weakened, not on life support, but *dead.* In our natural spiritual state, before we are born again, we are spiritually dead. *No one* is good enough to satisfy God's standard of moral perfection. We are so selfish, sinful, and polluted with sin that we don't even realize how sinful we are. Incredibly, we are able to look at ourselves in the mirror and think, *Now, there's a good person! That's someone who deserves to go to Heaven.* Yet we are spiritually dead.

If you are not a believer in Jesus Christ, you may feel your hackles rising. You might say, "What do you mean? I'm not dead! I'm vigorous. I'm alive. It's absurd to tell me I'm dead!"

Yet Jesus, in the parable of the prodigal son and the loving father, in Luke 15:11-32, explains how even the living can actually be dead. He tells the story of a father whose son leaves home, squanders his inheritance on sinful living, and returns home poor and repentant. And what does the father say? "This son of mine was dead and is alive again; he was lost and is found" (Luke 15:24). In his rebellious, sinful condition, the son was physically alive but spiritually dead. He had no fellowship with his father; he was lost. Only when he came home in repentance was he truly alive.

So it is with you and me. Before we repented of our sin and came home to God, we were dead; we were lost. The condition of every human being before coming to Jesus Christ is spiritual death. Everyone who lives without Jesus Christ is dead in his or her sins. Apart from salvation by grace through faith in Jesus Christ, we are nothing but walking corpses.

Paul writes, "God, who is rich in mercy, made us alive with Christ" (Ephesians 2:4-5). How did God make us alive with Christ? By giving us the *free gift* of salvation. As Paul writes, "It is by grace you have been saved, through faith— and this is not from yourselves, it is the gift of God—not by works, so that no one can boast" (Ephesians 2:8-9).

Now, the fact that salvation is a free gift is a problem for many people. Tragically, they are too proud to accept Christ's sacrifice on their behalf. They reject the offer of something they haven't earned all by themselves. They say, "I've worked hard for everything I've got—and I'm going to earn my way to Heaven with good works."

I like hardworking people who believe in earning everything they have. That's an admirable trait for this earthly life. But hard work won't get you into Heaven. You can't earn Heaven. You can't deserve Heaven. You can only receive Heaven as a free gift. Jesus paid for everything on the cross. All you have to do is stretch out your hand and accept it.

The first benefit of Heaven is that God raised us from the spiritual death into which we were born, and he makes us truly, eternally alive through spiritual rebirth.

Benefit #2: God's Mercy and Love

Because we are born into sin, and because we desire sin and continually commit sin, we have offended God. We may think we are good people, but our sins are truly detestable to our holy God. Every sin is an offense to him.

But Paul says that God has "great love for us," and he is "rich in mercy," despite our sinfulness (Ephesians 2:4). The late evangelist Luis Palau told a story about a mother in France who approached the emperor, Napoleon Bonaparte, asking him to pardon her son. Napoleon rejected her pleas, saying that the young man had committed his crime not once, but twice. The laws of France and the very notion of justice demanded that he be put to death.

"I'm not asking for justice," the mother said. "I'm pleading for mercy for my son."

"Your son does not deserve mercy," Napoleon said.

"If he deserved a pardon, it would not be mercy. And mercy is all I'm asking for."

Moved by her plea, Napoleon showed mercy—and he spared the young man's life.[1]

This mother taught the emperor the true meaning of mercy. We all deserve justice. We all deserve Hell. But God, in his great love for us, showed us mercy—undeserved grace and goodness—instead. The mercy and love of God are the second great benefit of Heaven.

Benefit #3: A Meaningful Life

God not only gives us life, he gives us a life worth living: "For we are God's handiwork, created in Christ Jesus to do good works, which God prepared in advance for us to do" (Ephesians 2:10). He made us alive with Christ, and gave us a life of good works—serving God, serving others, and preaching the good news of the Kingdom. He gave us meaningful work to do. He commissioned us to serve him and to serve others and to be witnesses for him in the neighborhood, on the campus, and at the workplace.

You've undoubtedly heard the phrase, "Get a life." It means "Stop being so annoying; go do something more interesting. Do something productive and responsible." For example, if your twentysomething son is living in your basement and playing video games all day long, it would be perfectly appropriate to tell him, "You need to go out and get a life."

When you were dead in your sins, you didn't have a life. But when you came to Christ in repentance and faith, when you were born again, God gave you this third wonderful benefit of Heaven. He gave you a meaningful life.

Benefit #4: A Purpose for Living

God has given us a life of purpose—the greatest purpose imaginable. Paul writes, "God raised us up with Christ and seated us with him in the heavenly realms in Christ Jesus, in order that in the coming ages he might show the incomparable riches of his grace, expressed in his kindness to us in Christ Jesus" (Ephesians 2:6-7).

When God saved us, he breathed life into us and awakened our dead spirits to a new purpose, an eternally important reason for living. What is our purpose for living? We are vibrant, visible, breathing demonstrations of God's character, of the amazing riches of his grace, expressed through his mercy and kindness to us in Christ Jesus.

As we go about our daily lives, we should live in a full awareness of God's purpose for us. At the office, in the neighborhood, on the campus, we should live mindfully as representatives of Heaven, as walking billboard advertisements of God's amazing grace, as ambassadors of King Jesus.

Paul says we have been seated with Jesus in the heavenly realms. We have a seat at the table of Heaven. You are on this earth, conducting your daily business, going to work, taking care of your family—but at the same time, you are seated in the heavenly realms. Wherever you go, whatever you do on this earth, you are a representative of Heaven. One of the greatest benefits of Heaven is that you have a heavenly purpose, right here, right now.

Benefit #5: Fulfilling Work to Do

God created us to do good works. Do those good works save us? No. As we saw earlier, salvation is "the gift of God—not by works, so that no one can boast" (Ephesians 2:8-9). No matter how many people we lead to Christ, no matter how many people we serve in his name, no matter how many churches we plant, no matter how many hospitals we build, our good works cannot save us. But that doesn't mean our works aren't valuable.

God gives us good works to do, and those good works benefit others and bring a sense of fulfillment and meaning to our lives. There's no unemployment line in the Kingdom of God. If you have been saved, if you are a child of God, then he has a fulfilling, enriching job for you to do. In fact, the Holy Spirit has given special gifts of ministry and service to all of God's children.

Most believers have multiple gifts in various combinations, and these gifts include (but are not limited to) gifts of administration, discernment, evangelism, exhortation, faith, giving, healing, helping, hospitality, knowledge, leadership, mercy, prophecy, serving, teaching, and wisdom.[2] The best way to discover your spiritual gifts is to get involved in ministry with other believers. They will likely be able to affirm certain gifts in you. For example, "I can see that you have the gift of leadership," or "You really have the gift of mercy."

Christians who are not exercising and using their gifts, who are not serving in the church and witnessing to their faith out in the world, are wasting the gifts God has given them. In many cases, people fail to use their gifts because they are timid, lacking in faith, or simply lazy. If you are not using your spiritual gifts, then you are not doing the fulfilling work that God prepared in advance for you to do. You are saying to God, "I don't care what gifts you've given me; I don't care what you've called me to do—I'm not going to do it. I choose disobedience and selfishness."

Imagine the heart of God as he watches one of his children spend day after day in selfish or meaningless pursuits. God created you to do good works. God saved you and gave you eternal life—and that means he has a claim on your life. You owe him everything you have and everything you are and everything you do.

God calls all believers to a life of good works in his name. He doesn't just call ministers and missionaries. He calls all believers to know him and to make him known. If you are a schoolteacher, a doctor, or a plumber, be a schoolteacher, doctor, or plumber for Jesus. Do your work as unto the Lord, and as a witness for the Lord. One of the great benefits of Heaven is that you are God's handiwork, created in Christ Jesus to do good works.

Benefit #6: Heavenly Citizenship

Earth is our temporary home. Heaven is our permanent home. "Our citizenship is in heaven. And we eagerly await a Savior from there, the Lord Jesus Christ" (Philippians 3:20). As citizens and ambassadors of Heaven, we are to live our lives as representatives of the Lord Jesus.

Far too many Christians take their citizenship in Heaven for granted. Some don't understand what citizenship in Heaven means, while others simply never think about it. But our citizenship in Heaven is a profoundly important biblical concept—a concept that would revolutionize our lives if we truly understood it.

As citizens of Heaven, we are to adopt Heaven's culture, values, and practices. Our way of life should stand in stark contrast to the way of this corrupt and dying world. The citizens of this world are obsessed with endless entertainment, acquiring wealth and status, and seeking security built on shrewd investments and fat 401(k) plans. As citizens of Heaven, our focus is to be on eternal things, and we should spend each day storing up treasure in Heaven.

As citizens of Heaven, we do not see ourselves as members of a political, racial, ethnic, or ideological tribe, but as ambassadors of Jesus Christ. We represent the King of Heaven and his Kingdom. Every decision we make is motivated and shaped by the fact that we are mere sojourners on this earth.

As citizens of Heaven, we do not make ourselves at home here on this planet, in this fallen age and this dying culture. We are seeking our true homeland. We desire a better country—a heavenly country. With our minds on Heaven, we continually talk about our King, Jesus. We urge everyone we meet to join us in that heavenly Kingdom.

Living as citizens of Heaven means we obey the commands of our King. When we see people who are hungry or thirsty, alone or alienated, needy or poor, sick or imprisoned, we reach out to them with the love of Jesus—the charity of our King. We live out the values of the Kingdom as radically transformed citizens of Heaven.

If that is how we truly saw ourselves every day, it would truly revolutionize the way we live our lives—from our first prayers of praise in the morning to our final words of thanks as we drift off to sleep. The whole world would take note and ask, "Why are *those* people so different?" The difference is simply this: Our citizenship is in Heaven.

Benefit #7: A Heavenly ID Card

Paul writes, "In Christ Jesus you who once were far away have been brought near by the blood of Christ" (Ephesians 2:13). What is our heavenly ID card? The blood of Christ.

As an earthly citizen, you undoubtedly carry an ID card. If you leave your home country and travel elsewhere, you must show a passport, which is your ID card. As a citizen of Heaven, you also have an ID card, a passport—and it is stamped by the indelible blood of Jesus Christ that was shed on the cross. The moment you came to Christ in repentance and faith, God gave you a new ID card that proclaims you a citizen of Heaven. If you try to claim that you are a citizen of Heaven on any other basis than the blood of Christ, you are offering a fake ID.

Make sure that the ID card you carry is genuine. Your genuine ID card, stamped with the blood of Jesus, will give you victory over sin and discouragement, temptation and opposition, not only in eternity but also here and now.

Benefit #8: A Daily Refuge of Peace

"For he himself is our peace," writes Paul, "who has made the two groups one and has destroyed the barrier, the dividing wall of hostility, by setting aside in his flesh the law with its commands and regulations. His purpose was to create in himself one new humanity out of the two, thus making peace" (Ephesians 2:14-15).

In the great Temple of Herod in Jerusalem, there was a warning carved in Greek lettering on a slab of limestone and painted with red paint. It read, "No foreigner [Gentile] is to enter within the balustrade and embankment around the sanctuary. Whoever is caught will have himself to blame for his death which follows."[3] Ancient historians Josephus and Philo recorded that, in order to keep the Jewish population happy, the Romans allowed the Sanhedrin to impose the death penalty on any Gentiles who violated this rule.

In our world today, there are many homes and hearts that are guarded with a warning: "No one may enter." As a result, many people live in lonely isolation, at war with the people around them, and even with the people in their own homes. But Jesus is our peace. When he reigns supreme in our lives, we will live in peace and unity.

Jesus came to a world of strife between Jews and Gentiles, and he made peace between them. Wherever you see racial strife, political strife, conflict between a husband and wife, or conflict in a church, it is always because Jesus is not reigning and ruling supreme over that relationship. Conflict results when sin has entered in and taken the place of Christ. Where Jesus reigns supreme, there is always peace. Under his rule, all hatred, prejudice, revenge, and strife will cease.

Jesus is our peace. There can be no peace unless Jesus reigns over our lives, our families, our churches, our communities, and our nation.

You may say, "I'm a believer, I'm a Christian, and my spouse is a Christian, yet our home is a war zone." Yes, you and your spouse may be Christians, but you're still allowing sin to control you. Your spouse says something that causes you to feel insulted or belittled or accused, so you feel you need to defend yourself, maybe even fight back. Instead of having the mind of Christ, you respond out of sin. You allow your selfishness and defensiveness to dominate your actions.

(Now, I'm speaking here of the ordinary conflicts and arguments that occur in families. But I need to make it clear that if there is harmful abuse being committed against you or your children, you have a responsibility to protect yourself and them from that abuse. Get out, get to a place that is safe, and get help.)

When Jesus was insulted, he did not fight back. When he was mocked, he did not retaliate. When he was accused, he did not defend himself. And when he was crucified, he said, "Father, forgive them, for they do not know what they are doing" (Luke 23:34). If Jesus reigns in your life, you will respond as Jesus responded. He will control your responses in times of conflict.

Benefit #9: A New and Loving Family

When Jesus became our peace, he abolished all hostility between us and God the Father—and between brothers and sisters in the church, fellow believers in Jesus Christ. Regardless of differences in race, language, economic status, or any other superficial differences, we are all one in Christ.

Jesus formed a new heavenly family on earth, with God as our Father and all other believers as our brothers and sisters. We have heavenly blood running through our veins. We are a family.

That's why Jesus tells us, "If your brother or sister sins, go and point out their fault, just between the two of you" (Matthew 18:15). Why does God want us to treat each other in this loving and peacemaking way? Why does he call us brothers and sisters? Because we are a family.

If Jesus presides over his family, then there will be peace. There won't always be agreement, but there will always be peace—and we will handle our disagreements as brothers and sisters in the Lord, not as enemies. Love transcends even our deepest disagreements.

The ninth benefit of Heaven is that we have a new and loving family in eternity—and in the here and now.

Benefit #10: A New Home

Paul tells us that God's Kingdom, his household of faith, is "built on the foundation of the apostles and prophets, with Christ Jesus himself as the chief cornerstone. In him the whole building is joined together and rises to become a holy temple in the Lord. And in him you too are being built together to become a dwelling in which God lives by his Spirit" (Ephesians 2:20-22).

Heaven is our new home, a building, a holy temple—and not only do we have a home in Heaven, but we *are* a home, a dwelling, in which God himself lives. The foundation of this home is made up of the Old Testament prophets and the New Testament apostles—and Jesus himself is the cornerstone which gives the entire foundation and dwelling its stability and strength. The walls and the roof of this dwelling rest firmly on that foundation—and without that foundation, the dwelling would fall.

The tenth benefit of Heaven is that we have been given a new home in which to dwell today and throughout eternity.

Don't Neglect the Benefits of Heaven

Many immigrants to the United States have become naturalized American citizens. They are now free to enjoy all the blessings of citizenship that a natural-born citizen enjoys. But there is one situation in which US citizenship can become a huge problem for naturalized American citizens—when they attempt to return to the land of their birth and that land is hostile to the United States.

Iranian-born American businessman Siamak Namazi is one of a number of US citizens who have suffered unfairly for attempting to visit the land of their birth. In October 2015, while Namazi was in Iran on business, he was arrested and detained in the notorious Evin Prison, where Iran punishes, tortures, and executes its dissidents and political prisoners. Because he had become a naturalized US citizen, Namazi was accused of "collaborating with enemy states."[4] To the government of Iran, if you were born an Iranian citizen, the state still has a claim on your loyalty.

I see a profound parallel between Mr. Namazi's plight as a US citizen imprisoned in the land of his birth and the plight of a citizen of Heaven who returns to his or her spiritual "native land." If you are a citizen of Heaven and you deliberately return to a state of sin and rebellion, carnality and disobedience, you are returning to Satan's territory from which Jesus saved you. By returning to Satan's territory, you have removed yourself from the protection of your heavenly citizenship.

I'm not saying that you will lose your salvation. I'm not saying you will lose your heavenly citizenship. You are still a citizen of your adopted heavenly country. The Bible does not teach that God writes your name in the Book of Life with a pencil, only to erase it when you fail. No, if you have truly committed your life to Jesus Christ, then your name is written in the Book of Life with the indelible blood of Jesus Christ. But if you rebel against Jesus and return to Satan's territory, you will bring pain and loss upon yourself. You will forgo the benefits of your heavenly citizenship.

If that is where you are right now, wandering in a wilderness of sin and rebellion, you can still repent. You can still return to a place of God's protection through your citizenship in Heaven.

Do not neglect the benefits of your heavenly citizenship. Treasure them. Enjoy them. Use those benefits to bless others and to spread the good news of the Kingdom.

4

THE BLESSINGS OF HEAVEN

A BBC PRODUCER WHO WAS PLANNING a series of broadcasts on what Christians believe asked a clergyman how he could determine the church's views on Heaven and Hell. The clergyman replied with a single word: "Die."

Though it's true that one could definitely find out the truth about Heaven and Hell by dying, there's a problem with that approach: If you have made the wrong choice between Heaven and Hell, it's too late to change your mind. There are no do-overs in eternity. As Hebrews 9:27 reminds us, "People are destined to die once, and after that to face judgment."

So we need to know what God's Word teaches us about

Heaven as early in life as possible, so that we can experience all the beauty, benefits, and blessings of Heaven in this life as well as in the next.

The Nine Blessings of Heaven

We have already looked at eight beautiful facets of Heaven and ten benefits of Heaven. Now we will look at nine blessings of Heaven—nine joyous advantages we will experience in the eternal presence of our Lord.

Blessing #1: No More Temptation

Once we get to Heaven, we will truly and finally be free. Free from opposition and temptation. Free from Satan's fiery darts. Free from Satan's attack on our relationships with others. Free from suspicion and resentment and misunderstanding. We'll be free from all sin.

In this life, we must struggle with the temptation to sin. God, through the active presence of the Holy Spirit in our lives, gives us the strength to say yes to God's will and no to temptation. But as long as we are in our un-resurrected bodies, temptation will always be a struggle and a curse in our lives. We have to pray daily, even hourly, those words from the prayer Jesus taught us: "Lead us not into temptation, but deliver us from the evil one" (Matthew 6:13).

But praise God, a day is coming when all of Satan's attacks, opposition, and temptations will come to an end. The ultimate victory over sin in our lives will finally be won.

When we arrive in Heaven, one of the most important blessings we will receive is this: no more temptation.

Blessing #2: No More Loss

Our lives on earth are blighted by change and loss. The people we love are taken away from us. Again and again, we encounter partings and separations. But not in Heaven. To arrive in Heaven is to arrive home. We will live in unity and community. The keynote of Heaven is joy. Loss, sorrow, bereavement—all these will be left behind.

There is nothing wrong with experiencing the emotion of grief when we suffer a loss. Nowhere does the Bible say that believers shouldn't grieve. But we "do not grieve like the rest of mankind, who have no hope" (1 Thessalonians 4:13).

When an unbeliever dies, the survivors are left with nothing but memories. But when a believing loved one dies, we have hope for the future. We believe in bodily resurrection and everlasting life. We know that death is merely a temporary separation. We are not saying "Goodbye forever," but, "Goodbye—until we meet again."

Yes, even a temporary separation is painful. We miss our children when they go off to college. We miss our parents when they retire and move to another state. It's only natural that we should miss our believing loved ones when they are promoted to eternal life in Heaven. We are suffering a loss—the loss of fellowship with people we love. So we grieve.

A time of loss is a time of looking back on good memories—but it's also a time of looking forward to a great reunion in Heaven. It is a time to remind ourselves of our own mortality. When we stand at the graveside of a loved one, we face the reality of death. We remember that a grave awaits us as well.

But a time of loss is no time to be morbid. The grave is not the end of the story. Our hope is in the empty tomb of the Lord Jesus Christ. We are confident that our bodies will be raised like his.

And death is not the only form of loss we suffer in this life. Loss comes to us in many shapes and forms. Sometimes, we must face the loss of a career. Or a marriage. Or a reputation. Or a dream. When we suffer any kind of loss, it is easy to tumble into despair and hopelessness.

I want you to know that the resurrected Jesus will conquer all of your losses. He will restore everything you have lost—and so much more—when you get to Heaven.

This earthly life is checkered with losses. We are constantly suffering the parting of ways. But when we arrive in Heaven, we will experience unity and community throughout eternity. We will live in total contentment—and we will never again suffer loss.

Blessing #3: No More Tears

Life on earth has been described as "a vale of tears" or "a valley of weeping." But Revelation 21:4 tells us that, in Heaven, God "will wipe every tear from their eyes. There will be no more death or mourning or crying or pain, for the old order of things has passed away."

Please understand, there is nothing wrong with shedding tears over the death of a loved one. The Bible acknowledges that it is normal to feel sorrow and emptiness when a loved one passes away. It is human to shed tears in times of sorrow.

The shortest verse in the Bible, John 11:35, is just two words long. It is also one of the most profound and meaningful verses in the Bible. When Jesus goes to the village of Bethany after the death of his friend Lazarus, the verse tells us, "Jesus wept."

The tears of Jesus spoke volumes to the people who heard him weep. "See how he loved him [Lazarus]!" they said.

When a deep and awful sadness overtakes us, it seems as if the entire world has come to a sudden halt. All the things that meant so much before—schedules, plans, entertainment, politics—suddenly become meaningless. It's hard to eat. It's hard to sleep. We don't feel like doing much of anything.

From a human perspective, the cross of Christ looked like a dead end. But on the first Easter Sunday, the cross became an open door to resurrection and redemption. The death of Jesus was not a loss but a victory, not an end but the beginning, not a setback but a breakthrough to eternity. Discouragement and despair cannot survive in the presence of the hope of Heaven.

The third blessing of Heaven is that all tears will be wiped away.

Blessing #4: No More Death

Death is a frightening and mysterious prospect that lies in wait for all of us. Even Christians cannot escape its shadow. But once we have passed through death and entered Heaven, death loses all its terror and sting. In Heaven, there will be no more death.

As believers, we must not allow ourselves to be infected by the world's fear of death. Because Jesus has passed through death, we know with certainty that death is not the end of life. Death is a change of address. We are simply moving from the basement to the penthouse. We are moving from the tent to the mansion. Once we are in Heaven, death vanishes into the past. It no longer has any power over us. We are safe from all dangers.

Once we are in Heaven, we never have to fear death again. We don't even have to think about it. Death has been vanquished. In Heaven, death itself dies. In Heaven, death is less than a memory and it is no longer in our future. In Heaven, death is powerless. In Heaven, we are home free.

Just thinking about Heaven and the end of death, I get so excited that I want to go to Heaven right now, before I even finish writing this sentence! I'm ready for Heaven, because the fourth blessing of Heaven is no more death!

Blessing #5: No More Regrets

Regret is one of the worst feelings in the world. "Oh, if only I had made a wiser decision!" "If only I had paid attention to the warning signs!" "If only I had said those words when there was still time!" "If only I could take back those words I spoke so carelessly." "If only I had realized the terrible mistake I was making!" "If only I could live my life over again!"

We all have regrets. You have them and so do I. Our words and actions have consequences, and those consequences usually cannot be undone.

But God has made it possible for us to let go of our regrets. He offers us forgiveness and grace for our sins, failures, and self-blame in this life. In the next life, he offers us Heaven, a place where there will be no more regrets.

When we arrive in Heaven, we will turn the page. All our unkind words and actions will be forgotten. All our selfish and sinful deeds will be remembered no more. God has expunged our record and wiped away all of our guilt and regrets. Our sins and failures will be forgotten things of the past.

Blessing #6: No More Separation

In Revelation 21:1, John writes, "Then I saw 'a new heaven and a new earth,' for the first heaven and the first earth had passed away, and there was no longer any sea." To John, the sea represented separation. He experienced his vision while he was exiled on the island of Patmos, where the Roman Empire maintained a military garrison.

When John stood on the shores of that island and looked across the Aegean Sea, he probably thought about all the friends on the mainland, over the horizon, beyond his view. He was separated from them by the sea. In his mind, the phrase "there was no longer any sea" was likely synonymous with "there will be no more separation."

As believers, we need to continually remind ourselves of how breathtakingly beautiful it will be to spend eternity in the presence of God. We will have glorious fellowship with our Lord and with each other—and there will be no more separation.

Blessing #7: No More Schedules

One of the great curses of twenty-first century American life is that we are overstressed, overcommitted, and over-scheduled. We don't take time to reflect on the things that mean the most in life—especially our relationship with the Lord Jesus Christ. We are driven by deadlines. Even when we go on vacation, we have to keep to our tightly planned itinerary, so that we come back from vacation more exhausted and stressed than when we left.

Hurrying and scheduling can be ruthless taskmasters—and they can hinder our spiritual life and our life of service to others. We need to learn right now how to live in greater alignment with Heaven. And in Heaven there will be no more schedules.

Our busy schedules shouldn't keep us from giving our full attention to our children when they need us. Our busy schedules shouldn't keep us from sharing the gospel with a friend or running an errand for a sick neighbor. Our busy schedules shouldn't keep us from ministering to the needs of someone who is helpless, hopeless, or in need of a Christian friend.

Jesus was never too busy to stop and meet a spiritual or physical need. He lived the lifestyle of the Kingdom of Heaven—a lifestyle that placed people ahead of schedules. And we should live the lifestyle of Heaven as well.

In Revelation 21:23, John writes that Heaven "does not need the sun or the moon to shine on it, for the glory of God gives it light, and the Lamb is its lamp." We will no longer live our lives by the rising of the sun or the phases of the moon. All the illumination we need will come from God the Father and his Son, Jesus Christ.

We will have all of eternity to enjoy, and we will no longer have to earn our daily bread by the sweat of our brow. We will be freed from enslavement to time and the clock and schedules and deadlines. We will be freed from endless meetings and phone calls and production quotas. We will not be dashing from one appointment to another. We will live an unhurried life, and there will be plenty of time for everything.

Blessing #8: No More Darkness

In Rome, you can see the dungeon at the Mamertine Prison, where the apostle Paul is believed to have been confined. It was originally dug as a cistern for a natural spring. There was no possibility of escape because it was a cavelike place and prisoners were lowered into it through a hole in the ceiling. Food and water were lowered to the prisoners through that same hole.

The Mamertine Prison was a place of horrifying, claustrophobic darkness. There were no windows, no doors, only deep shadows and even deeper despair. But Paul was not defeated by his prison cell. Though he was physically confined, his spirit was free to commune with God.

At the end of Paul's imprisonment, he was taken to a place of execution. The moment after he drew his last earthly breath, he joined the Lord Jesus in Heaven. In the midst of his darkness, Paul never lost hope because he knew he was going to a place of infinite and eternal light.

In Heaven, there is no more darkness. Not only will God banish the darkness of night, but he will also banish the darkness of ignorance, misunderstanding, anger, hate, and resentment.

Sometimes the behavior of other people mystifies us. Sometimes even our own behavior mystifies us. Why do we so often sin when we really want to obey the Lord? The dark and mysterious depths of human motives and behavior will all be exposed to the light—and in Heaven there will be no more human darkness. As Paul put it, "Now I know in part; then I shall know fully, even as I am fully known" (1 Corinthians 13:12).

The eighth blessing of Heaven is no more darkness—of any kind.

Blessing #9: No More Disillusionment

One of the most difficult realities of this life is the experience of disappointment, discouragement, and disillusionment. Even though we know and love Jesus, we sometimes find ourselves questioning God: "Lord, why is this prayer going unanswered?" "Lord, why does my life seem so meaningless right now?" "Lord, I'm trying to follow you and obey you, yet everything in my life is falling apart."

In the book of Ecclesiastes, Solomon—probably the most successful and accomplished human being who ever lived—came to a point in his life where he concluded: "Meaningless! Meaningless! . . . Utterly meaningless! Everything is meaningless" (Ecclesiastes 1:2).

Our best efforts and our loftiest achievements can leave us disappointed and disillusioned. Yes, we experience moments on the mountaintop, but we spend most of our lives toiling in the deep valleys of life.

But all of that will disappear from our lives the moment we enter Heaven. Life will no longer be empty and meaningless. We will be busy reigning and ruling with Christ forever and ever.

So let's be gratefully amazed by the beauty and benefits and blessings of our eternal home in Heaven. Let's daily remind ourselves of the deep meaning of the words Jesus taught us to pray: "Our Father in heaven, hallowed be your name, your kingdom come, your will be done, on earth as it is in heaven" (Matthew 6:9-10).

When Jesus taught us to pray to the Father in Heaven, he was raising our eyes to behold God's greatness, majesty, and power. The infinite resources of Heaven will satisfy all our needs. That's why James tells us, "Every good and perfect gift is from above, coming down from the Father of the heavenly lights, who does not change like shifting shadows"

(James 1:17). God can see all that is happening in our lives—
and he can influence those events for our benefit.

Yet, though your Father is in Heaven, he is as close to you
as your own beating heart. Thank God for his nearness to
you, even as he is in Heaven watching over you and preparing
a place for you.

Even though this world seems totally out of control, God
in Heaven is in total control. He rules the universe with an
all-encompassing precision that vastly exceeds the understanding of our greatest human minds. He listens from
Heaven when we pray, and he pours out the blessings of
Heaven whenever we need them.

Where Your Treasure Is

The Bible mentions Heaven about five hundred times.
Shouldn't we in the church be investing more sermons, more
Bible studies, and more everyday conversations in the subject
of Heaven? As Jesus said, "Store up for yourselves treasures in
heaven, where moths and vermin do not destroy, and where
thieves do not break in and steal. For where your treasure
is, there your heart will be also" (Matthew 6:20-21). If your
treasure is not in Heaven, then your heart is not in Heaven
either.

Focusing on Heaven produces godliness in our lives here
and now. A focus on Heaven brings us joy and comfort in the
midst of trials. Focusing on Heaven places our earthly pain
and suffering in an eternal perspective. Focusing on Heaven
empowers us to live in victory over temptation and sin.

Keep Heaven in your sights as you journey through this temporary, transitory life. Let the beauty of Heaven thrill you. Let the benefits of Heaven inspire you. Let the blessings of Heaven excite you.

Look forward to Heaven. Never lose sight of your eternal destiny. Eagerly anticipate Heaven's beauty, benefits, and blessings.

the UNFOLDING of HEAVEN

part 2

5

WHO GOES TO HEAVEN?

THERE'S NO SHORTAGE of Hollywood films about Heaven.

One of the earliest was *Here Comes Mr. Jordan* in 1941, about a boxer who was taken to Heaven by mistake and then was given a second chance at life on earth.

In 1943, Spencer Tracy starred in *A Guy Named Joe*, about a WWII pilot who was killed in a plane crash but gets to return to earth to help the people he loves. (This film was remade by Steven Spielberg in 1989 as *Always*, starring Richard Dreyfuss.)

Also in 1943, Hollywood released *Heaven Can Wait*, in which a sinful man dies, expecting to go to Hell; but after recounting his life story, he is sent to Heaven instead. A very different *Heaven Can Wait* was made in 1978, starring Warren Beatty.

In 1998, Robin Williams starred in *What Dreams May Come* as a grieving husband who rescues his wife from Hell.

What do all these movies about Heaven have in common? They all ignore what the Bible teaches about Heaven and what Jesus himself teaches about Heaven.

There is probably no subject that people are more confused about than who goes to Heaven and how we get there. There are so many conflicting views and opinions that it seems most people make up their minds based on their wishes or what somebody said on daytime TV.

Satan's Depiction of Heaven

Because of the many Hollywood movies about the afterlife, silly notions about Heaven abound. Many think that everyone who dies goes to Heaven. Or that people who die become angels. Or that Heaven is a place where people sit on clouds, dressed in white robes, strumming harps. If you want to know what Heaven is *really* like, avoid the Hollywood versions and go straight to the truth of God's Word.

Atheists and agnostics will try to convince you that Heaven is a myth and Hell is a cruel lie meant to scare you. They tell us that when we die, there's no soul, no afterlife, no Heaven, no Hell, no resurrection. They claim that, at the moment of death, everything we were while we were alive becomes ashes and dust—just so much dead matter.

The late science fiction writer and atheist Isaac Asimov put it this way: "Since I am an atheist . . . I can only suppose that when I die, there will only be an eternity of nothingness to follow. . . . There is nothing frightening about an eternal dreamless sleep. Surely it is better than eternal torment in Hell or eternal boredom in Heaven."[1] As I read those words, my heart breaks for this poor, deceived man. And I fear for so many other people who have fallen for Satan's depiction of Heaven as a place of *eternal boredom*!

Most people, when asked if they will go to Heaven when they die, say something like, "Well, I *hope* so," or, "I think my good deeds will outweigh my bad deeds, so yes, that should get me into Heaven," or, "I'm not perfect, but I've lived a good life, so I think I'll go to Heaven," or, "I think so. I'm not a religious person, but I live by the Golden Rule," or, "I'm not religious, but I'm spiritual. I'll either go to Heaven or I'll be reincarnated."

The problem with these opinions is that they're all self-centered. In the final analysis, it doesn't matter what we wish for. It doesn't matter what Hollywood portrays or what some "spiritual" guru claims in his latest bestseller. The only thing that matters is what God says in his Word. What Jesus said to a Pharisee named Nicodemus—and to you and me—is this: "Very truly I tell you, no one can see the kingdom of God unless they are born again" (John 3:3).

When Jesus speaks of "the kingdom of God," he is using an alternate term for Heaven, where Jesus will rule supreme as the King of kings throughout eternity.

Satan constantly tries to rob us of the hope and joy of

Heaven. He distorts the image of Heaven and makes believers afraid of death and eternity. He slanders Heaven as a boring place where no one would ever want to go.

Why does Satan lie about Heaven? Why does he cause some people to dread Heaven as a place of perpetual boredom? The answer is obvious: Satan lies about Heaven because he was thrown out of Heaven—and he can never go back. But *we* will go to Heaven if we are followers of Jesus.

That's why Satan hates God and why he hates us—we're going to Heaven and he's not. Every time Satan lies to you or attacks you, simply turn around and taunt him: "I'm going to Heaven and you're not!"

What Does It Mean to Be Born Again?

What does the phrase "born again" mean? Throughout most of the twentieth century, the term was rarely heard outside of Christian circles. In the 1960s, many Jesus People, members of the Christian counterculture, began to announce themselves as "born again." In 1976, the redeemed and reformed Watergate conspirator Charles Colson published the story of his Christian conversion and titled it *Born Again*. That same year, Georgia governor Jimmy Carter (who was also a Baptist Sunday school teacher) announced that he was running for president and that he was a "born again Christian."[2]

The secular media found the notion of being "born again" as baffling and incomprehensible as Nicodemus did two thousand years earlier. Journalists reported on the "born-again" Christianity of Charles Colson and Jimmy Carter in terms that ranged from puzzlement to outright scorn. Many Christians who had once declared themselves born again felt intimidated by how the anti-Christian media jeered and mocked the term. So they began to shy away from calling themselves born again.

But let's be clear: "Born again" is not a phrase invented by the church or Charles Colson or Jimmy Carter or the anti-Christian media. Jesus himself coined the phrase as a description of what it really means to be a saved follower of his. We must not let the secular media redefine this beautiful description of the reality of salvation.

The Lord Jesus said that only those who are born again shall see Heaven, shall enter into Heaven, shall live eternally in Heaven. So it's vitally important that every human being on the planet discover what this term means.

Jesus is God. He coexisted with the Father before the world was created. He came from Heaven to Earth to save us from our sins and reconcile us to God the Father. And Jesus said that no one can enter into Heaven unless they are born again. So it is supremely important that we understand what Jesus meant. And once we know what it means to be born again, we have a decision to make. We must either accept or reject being born again.

So what does it mean to be born again? Let's see what Jesus meant when he spoke these strange and profound words.

Nicodemus: Seeking Jesus in the Darkness

In John 3, Jesus meets a man named Nicodemus, who comes to him under cover of darkness. Nicodemus was a prominent man in society—learned and deeply religious. He had probably memorized much of the Old Testament. He kept the ceremonial laws of the Old Testament. He even kept the detailed, ritualized, man-made interpretations of the ceremonial laws.

Why, then, did he come to Jesus at all? The answer is clear: All of his outward religiosity had failed to give him real satisfaction in life. He was hungry for truth, for meaning, for reality, for joy. His heart was dissatisfied, his mind was seeking. When he saw Jesus, he saw someone who had the power of God coursing through him. Jesus healed the sick and raised the dead and fed the hungry—and he never asked to be paid for these wonderful deeds.

Most important of all, Jesus was a man who demonstrated heavenly authority. He claimed to forgive sins. He spoke about the Kingdom of Heaven. He never quoted any scribes or rabbis. He said, "I say to you." He spoke from his own authority, as if he had authority from God himself. Because he did.

So Nicodemus came to Jesus because he was convinced that Jesus was not just another teacher. Jesus was someone with authority from Heaven.

But Nicodemus was not yet willing to admit that he needed to be saved from his sins. He was still trying to protect his reputation as a morally superior and religious man. That's why he came to see Jesus at night. He didn't want anyone to see him and say, "Oh, look at Nicodemus! He's becoming a Jesus freak."

Nicodemus came in secret because he longed to know the truth. The question that haunted him was: "If I die, will I go to Heaven?"

He struggled with emptiness and apprehension in his life. All his religious observance was not helping him. All the rituals of Judaism did not satisfy him. All the traditions seemed dead and meaningless.

So Nicodemus came to Jesus and said, "Rabbi, we know that you are a teacher who has come from God. For no one could perform the signs you are doing if God were not with him" (John 3:2).

Who was this "we" that Nicodemus referred to when he said, "We know that you are a teacher who has come from God"? Nicodemus was not alone among the members of the Sanhedrin (the Supreme Court of Israel at the time) to recognize Jesus' power and authority. They suspected that the signs Jesus performed might be evidence that he was the long-awaited Messiah.

But the members of the Sanhedrin were afraid of peer pressure. They were afraid of what other powerful men might think of them. They were afraid of being canceled by the cancel culture of first-century Israel.

The Infinite Importance of Eternal Life

One of the great spiritual tragedies of that day—and of our time as well—is that people allow their fear of peer pressure to keep them out of the Kingdom of Heaven. They don't want people to judge them or mock them for being Jesus freaks, so they deny Christ and doom themselves to an eternity without him.

Please understand: Your eternal life is infinitely more important than anything people say about you or think about you. Your eternal life is infinitely more important than what people may do to you, even if they would persecute you or kill you.

Don't be intimidated by people. Don't be afraid of peer pressure. Seek Jesus and his Kingdom because Jesus loves you. Even if your peers don't love you, Jesus does.

When Nicodemus came to Jesus by night, Jesus told him, "Very truly I tell you, no one can see the kingdom of God unless they are born again" (John 3:3).

Nicodemus came to Jesus with words of praise and commendation. He called him "Rabbi," a term of honor. He said that he recognized Jesus as a teacher sent from God, because no one could perform such great works without the power of God. But Jesus ignored those compliments and zeroed in on what was infinitely more important: Nicodemus needed to be born again.

If you were raised in a family where religious rituals and traditions were extremely important, you might have thought that those rituals and traditions could save you. If so, then you can identify with Nicodemus. Jesus had to shake up this man's worldview. He had to make Nicodemus understand that rituals and traditions are meaningless without a completely transformed heart.

To be saved, you must be born again.

Born of Water and the Spirit

When Jesus told Nicodemus that he needed to be born again, it was as if Jesus had triggered a bomb under everything this man believed, everything he lived for, everything he had built his life on. Nicodemus had relied on his own good works, his own keeping of the law of Moses and all the manmade rituals and traditions that had been added to the law.

But Jesus said, "You must be born again."

Boom! Everything Nicodemus had lived for was blown to pieces.

Born again? What does *that* mean?

So Nicodemus, a very literal-minded Pharisee, asked Jesus, "How can someone be born when they are old? Surely they cannot enter a second time into their mother's womb to be born!" (John 3:4).

For the second time, Jesus begins his reply with the phrase, "Very truly."

"Very truly I tell you, no one can enter the kingdom of God unless they are born of water and the Spirit. Flesh gives birth to flesh, but the Spirit gives birth to spirit. You should not be surprised at my saying, 'You must be born again'" (John 3:5-7).

"Very truly" (or "Verily, verily," as many older English translations render it) is a statement of emphasis. Jesus was trying to get Nicodemus to pay close attention. He was about to tell him the truth, the whole truth, and nothing but the truth.

Jesus told Nicodemus—and you and me—that, in order

to go to Heaven, we must allow God to do something to us. We must allow God to transform us and completely change us. We cannot make ourselves acceptable to God by keeping religious rituals or trying to live a good life. We cannot simply make cosmetic changes. No, we must be *radically transformed*. We must be born again.

This second birth is a spiritual transformation—a transformation that is carried out by the Holy Spirit.

What does Jesus mean when he says that "no one can enter the kingdom of God unless they are born of water and the Spirit"? Jesus is referring to God's Old Testament proclamation through the prophet Ezekiel: "I will sprinkle clean water on you, and you will be clean; I will cleanse you from all your impurities and from all your idols. I will give you a new heart and put a new spirit in you; I will remove from you your heart of stone and give you a heart of flesh. And I will put my Spirit in you and move you to follow my decrees and be careful to keep my laws" (Ezekiel 36:25-27).

Ezekiel spoke of a time to come when God would give his people a transformational new beginning. The symbols of that new beginning are "water and the Spirit." Water cleanses us of all sin, idolatry, and impurity. The Holy Spirit transforms our hearts, taking away our hearts of stone and giving us new, softened hearts of flesh, so that we can walk in the Spirit and follow God's decrees.

That is what it means to be born again, to be born of water and the Spirit. It is not a concept that Jesus invented in his conversation with Nicodemus. It's a promise that God the Father made through the Old Testament prophet Ezekiel six centuries before the birth of Jesus.

Who has been born again? A born-again person is one who has been radically transformed by Jesus, whose life has been invaded by the power of the Holy Spirit, who is living for Jesus in this life, and who is going to Heaven in the next.

Who is going to Heaven? All those who have experienced a new beginning in life by being "born of water and the Spirit." All those who have been cleansed by God and have been given a new heart and a new indwelling Spirit.

A Deep Hunger

During the eighteenth century, John Wesley founded the Methodist movement, which began in the Church of England and eventually became the independent Methodist denomination that continues today. As an evangelistic preacher, Wesley chose John 3:7 as his favorite Bible text: "You must be born again." He preached on this passage countless times in England, Ireland, and America.

One day, a man approached him and asked, "Why do you preach so often on 'you must be born again'?"

"Because," Wesley replied, "you must be born again."[3]

Nicodemus came to Jesus with a deep hunger. He didn't know what could satisfy that hunger, but he knew that Jesus had the answer. What Nicodemus didn't know was that Jesus *is* the answer to that hunger. Jesus is so much more than a rabbi or spiritual teacher—he is the Lord; he is the Savior.

Nicodemus had a discontentment in his life and only

Jesus could settle it. Jesus didn't waste any time debating with him or receiving his compliments. He went straight to the root of Nicodemus's problem. He didn't need to be improved. He didn't need to be motivated to live a better life. He didn't need a new religion or belief system. He needed radical transformation. He needed to be born again.

The phrase "born again" puzzled Nicodemus. He wondered how an old man—or anyone at any age—could return to the womb and be born again. Nicodemus's puzzlement gave Jesus an opening to explain to him a reality that he should have understood from his training in the Old Testament. Jesus was telling him that trying harder isn't the answer and keeping the law isn't the answer. The problem is not what we do, but *who* and *what* we are.

That's why self-improvement is not enough. We need radical transformation. We need a complete rebirth.

Only Jesus can transform us. Only Jesus can fill our lives with purpose and meaning. Only Jesus can assure us of eternal life. Only him.

We are all born with the sin of Adam encoded in our spiritual DNA. Every human being who has ever lived has been born with an inherent sin problem. That sin problem is what nailed Jesus to the cross until he died and satisfied the Father's justice. He was buried in a tomb. Then, on the third day, he arose in triumph over death and the grave.

When we commit our lives to Jesus, when we are born again, we become new creatures, we become radically transformed. This doesn't mean we will never sin again. It doesn't

WHO GOES TO HEAVEN?

mean that we will never struggle against sinful habits and temptation. We will. In fact, as Paul writes, "I do not do the good I want to do, but the evil I do not want to do—this I keep on doing" (Romans 7:19). However, he continues, "If I do what I do not want to do, it is no longer I who do it, but it is sin living in me that does it" (Romans 7:20). Sin still lives in our dead flesh, but our born-again self struggles to overcome it. We rely on the Holy Spirit to resist sin, and we confess and repent of our sin whenever it rears up in our lives.

When I was a young man, I repeatedly tried and failed to overcome sin in my life. I kept telling myself, "The next time I'm tempted, I'll try harder and I'll do better." But I was never able to keep that promise—until March 4, 1964. That's when I asked Jesus to become the Lord of my life. That's when the Holy Spirit of God entered my life and I became born again.

In order to be born again, we must first admit we have a problem that needs solving. We must admit that we are sinners, we deserve everlasting punishment, we are headed for Hell, and we are incapable of saving ourselves from our own sin. We must recognize our lost condition.

Everyone who wants to go to Heaven must understand that Heaven cannot be earned. We can't do anything to deserve being saved. If we try to convince ourselves that we are good enough to satisfy a holy God, that our good works can qualify us to get into Heaven, we are fooling ourselves.

That's not just my *opinion*. It's the undeniable truth that Jesus himself stated: "Very truly I tell you, no one can enter the kingdom of God unless they are born of water and the Spirit" (John 3:5).

The One Thing That Keeps People Out of Heaven

In all my decades of Christian ministry, I have observed one universal factor that keeps people out of Heaven. I have seen it over and over, all around the world, in culture after culture. That one factor is people's unwillingness to admit they are sinners.

Again and again, I've heard people say, "Me? A sinner? No, no, no, I'm a good person! I've never done anything that deserves eternal punishment. I don't claim to be perfect, but a sinner? Absolutely not. I don't need Jesus to die for my sins. I am perfectly capable of living a good life, of making myself acceptable to God. I don't need to be born again. I can get to Heaven on my own good works, thank you very much!"

Please hear me. Until you let go of the delusion that you are morally good, that you are good enough to be accepted by God, that your good works somehow outweigh your bad works, you will delude yourself straight into an eternity apart from God. You will shut yourself outside of his Kingdom.

The ancient Egyptians believed that their lives would be weighed on a set of cosmic scales. The heart (with its good and bad deeds) was put on one side of the scale and weighed against the "feather of truth" on the other side. If one's good deeds outweighed the bad, that person would be accepted by the gods and go to Aaru, the heavenly Field of Reeds.

But Jesus came with a starkly different message about

Heaven. He said that God doesn't weigh our good deeds against our sins. Instead, God offers us completely transformed lives through spiritual rebirth. Jesus said we must be born again to enter the Kingdom of Heaven.

God has produced that spiritual rebirth in countless lives, including my own. He longs to produce that spiritual rebirth in your life today. God alone can re-create you. The God who created Adam from dust can make a completely new creature out of you.

The Sovereign Wind and the Sovereign Spirit

Jesus goes on to say, "The wind blows wherever it pleases. You hear its sound, but you cannot tell where it comes from or where it is going. So it is with everyone born of the Spirit" (John 3:8). Here Jesus uses a play on words, based on the Hebrew *ruach*, which means *breath*, *wind*, or *spirit*.

The wind is sovereign and blows wherever it wishes, just like the Holy Spirit. Nobody can tell the wind where to go. Nobody can tell the hurricane where to go. And just as we cannot predict the wind, we cannot control the Holy Spirit, the sovereign Spirit of God, who moves wherever he wishes and accomplishes whatever he chooses.

Nicodemus, as a religious scholar, should have understood that the Old Testament foretold that the Messiah would bring a message of spiritual rebirth and a new heart. But the Spirit had not yet opened Nicodemus's eyes.

So Jesus said, "You are Israel's teacher, and do you not understand these things? Very truly I tell you, we speak of what we know, and we testify to what we have seen, but still you people do not accept our testimony. I have spoken to you of earthly things and you do not believe; how then will you believe if I speak of heavenly things?" (John 3:10-12).

A friend of mine who recently gave his life to the Lord told me, "Before I committed my life to Jesus Christ as my Savior, I would read the Bible and I couldn't understand it. But when the Holy Spirit came into my life, I would read the passages that had mystified me before and suddenly I understood them!"

As a Pharisee, Nicodemus had studied and memorized vast passages of the Old Testament. He knew them by heart—yet he didn't understand what they meant because he didn't have the Holy Spirit to awaken his understanding.

The Serpent and the Savior

Jesus referred to a specific Old Testament text in Numbers 21, which Nicodemus should have understood. The Israelites were stuck in the wilderness for forty years due to their hardened hearts toward God. They complained against God, even after he delivered them from slavery in Egypt. So God sent fiery serpents to bite them. The people could not be cured except by God's direct intervention.

God told Moses to make a bronze serpent and lift it high so that anyone who looked at it would live. This serves as a powerful reminder that only God can deliver us from sin and take us to Heaven, just as only God could deliver the Israelites from the deadly serpent bite.

Moses obediently made a bronze serpent so that the people could look at it and be healed. Was there power in that bronze serpent? No. The power was not in the serpent but in the obedience of the people who looked up to it.

Many people today think it's foolish to believe that Jesus died on the cross for our sins. Yet it's the power of the cross that saves us and brings eternal healing. It's the power of the cross that will take us to Heaven.

Why did God order Moses to lift up a bronze serpent in the wilderness? Why a serpent and not some other symbol? In the Bible, a serpent has always been associated with sin. When Satan tempted Adam and Eve and brought doubt and temptation to their minds, he spoke through a serpent.

Because the serpent is associated with sin in the Bible, that bronze serpent represented Jesus, who became our sin, crucified on the cross, so that we can receive eternal healing when we look to him in faith.

There were undoubtedly some people who did not look at the bronze serpent in the wilderness. Maybe they said, "I've just been bitten by a venomous snake—and Moses says that if I look at a bronze sculpture I'll be healed? What foolishness!" Unfortunately, anyone who took that attitude died. But everyone who looked at the bronze serpent in obedience was healed.

In the same way, only those who come to Jesus in repentance and faith will be assured of Heaven. Faith in Christ sounds like foolishness to some—and they refuse to accept his free gift of forgiveness and spiritual rebirth. But everyone who looks to Jesus in faith will be healed and forgiven. It has nothing to do with how good you are. It has everything to do with the infinite worth of Jesus' sacrifice on the cross.

Standing in the Place of Nicodemus

Decades ago, I had a conversation with a woman—let's call her Mrs. Franklin. She was struggling with doubts about Heaven. She told me, "I believe in Jesus and I believe in God—but deep down, I'm not sure I really believe in Heaven. I don't know for sure that I'm going to Heaven when I die."

I said, "What do you mean, you believe in Jesus and God? I believe in America and I believe in the existence of bread—but neither of these beliefs will save me. What kind of belief do you have in Jesus and God?"

She said, "I have committed my life to Jesus as my Lord and Savior. I believe that I'm a sinner and that Jesus died for my sins. I believe that God the Father has forgiven my sins because of the sacrifice of his Son, Jesus. But I still have a hard time believing that I'm going to Heaven."

I knew this dear woman had a saving faith in Jesus, even though she struggled with doubts about Heaven. I prayed for wisdom, and God gave me an insight to share with her.

"Mrs. Franklin," I said, "when did your name change? When did you cease to be Miss So-and-So and become Mrs. Franklin?"

She said, "On my wedding day."

"What happened on your wedding day?"

"I took my wedding vows."

"Did you say, 'I *hope* to take you, Mr. Franklin, to be my husband'? or 'I would like to take you, Mr. Franklin, to be my husband, even though I'm not sure it will work out'?"

"Of course not! I said, 'I do.' I meant it, and it was final."

"Mrs. Franklin, that's how eternal life works. When you look at that cross and say to Jesus, 'I take you, Jesus, to be my only Lord and Savior,' everything changes. Not just in this life, but throughout eternity in Heaven. It's final. You have experienced a spiritual rebirth. You *are* going to Heaven, no doubt about it."

And that explanation completely transformed Mrs. Franklin's understanding of her present faith—and her future in Heaven with Jesus.

You may be experiencing a void, a restlessness, or a sense of meaninglessness within. Only Jesus can fill that void. Only when you come to him, confessing that you are a sinner in need of salvation, will he fill that void.

You have a deep hunger that religious activities and good works cannot fill. You are in the same place Nicodemus was when he came to Jesus by night. And the answer Jesus has for you is the same answer he gave to Nicodemus: *You must be born again.*

6

THE THREE HEAVENS

IN 1271, AN ITALIAN MERCHANT and explorer named Marco Polo left the city-state of Venice and journeyed east through Persia, India, China, and Mongolia. There he immersed himself in many foreign cultures and met such remarkable people as Emperor Kublai Khan of China and the Mongolian princess Kököchin. He recorded his findings and adventures in a memoir titled *Book of the Marvels of the World*. The stories and wonders contained in that book are true—yet the customs and cultures he described seemed so strange that his original readers thought he had made it all up. Even his family and friends thought he had invented most of his stories, and they nicknamed him *Il Milione* ("the million"), thinking he was a man of a million lies.

In December 1323, Marco Polo became seriously ill. He grew weaker and weaker, and by early January 1324, his family called the Catholic priest to hear his confession and administer last rites. The priest urged him to confess that he had made up the many marvelous tales in his book, but Marco Polo refused to recant his stories. "I did not tell half of what I saw," he said, "for I knew I would not be believed."[1]

Marco Polo's experience reminds me of the apostle Paul, who (referring to himself in the third person) recalled "visions and revelations from the Lord" in which he was taken to "the third heaven." There, he "heard inexpressible things, things that no one is permitted to tell" (2 Corinthians 12:1-2, 4). In other words, Paul didn't tell half of what he saw and heard in Heaven, because these things were impossible to put into words—and forbidden to be spoken.

If you have ever read this passage before, you may have been baffled by Paul's reference to "the third heaven." You may have wondered how many heavens there are, and what's the difference between them.

Throughout my years in ministry, I have been troubled by the great amount of confusion that exists—including in the church—regarding Heaven. I have found that many Christians find the subject so confusing that they don't even want to think about Heaven.

I remember in my youth reading about Soviet cosmonaut Yuri Gagarin, the first man to orbit the earth. According to some newspaper accounts at the time, after Gagarin returned to earth, he announced, "I went up to space, but I didn't

encounter God." For years, I felt sorry for this Soviet space-
man who returned to earth confirmed in his atheism.

Only recently did I learn that Yuri Gagarin never uttered
those words. In fact, it was Soviet Premier Nikita Khrushchev,
in a speech to the Soviet Central Committee, who claimed
that Gagarin never saw God in space. The quote became
attributed to Gagarin, but one of his closest friends says it
could not have been true. Why? Because Yuri Gagarin was a
devout Russian Orthodox Christian. Khrushchev was merely
spreading atheist propaganda—and because of the persecution of Christians by the Soviets, Gagarin kept silent and
didn't contradict the Soviet premier.[2]

I am thrilled to hear that Yuri Gagarin was a believer. The
state-sponsored atheism of the old Soviet Union was a tool of
Satan to keep millions of people in spiritual darkness.

Yet even in the church, the subject of Heaven is cloaked
in darkness, ignorance, and confusion. If you ask a professing
Christian, "When you die, will you go to Heaven?" many
reply, "I hope so." They have no certainty, no assurance. They
have only a vague, tentative hope.

When do most of us think about Heaven? When a loved
one dies. During the funeral service or at the graveside, the
question of Heaven becomes very real and urgent. But in
the days following the funeral, the reality of Heaven and the
urgency of Heaven quickly fade from our minds as the hurry
and pressures of daily life crowd back in.

If we know the Lord, Heaven is where we will spend eternity. It seems only reasonable, then, that we would want to

know everything we can learn about Heaven. After all, we are not just planning a vacation, we are planning our entire afterlife in eternity.

Minds Occupied with Heaven

Make no mistake about it, Heaven is not a vague, ghostly place somewhere in the clouds. Heaven is a physical place— and it is a breathtakingly beautiful place. Studying about Heaven, planning for Heaven, and focusing on Heaven should be the greatest motivation imaginable for living out our everyday lives. All the apostles lived with their gaze focused on Heaven. All the persecuted martyrs of the early church died with the hope of Heaven on their lips and in their hearts.

The apostle Peter said that when "the day of the Lord" comes, the heavens and the earth will be destroyed by the fire of God's judgment (2 Peter 3:10). "But in keeping with his promise," Peter continues, "we are looking forward to a new heaven and a new earth, where righteousness dwells. So then, dear friends, since you are looking forward to this, make every effort to be found spotless, blameless and at peace with him" (2 Peter 3:13-14).

Do you see how Peter links the hope of Heaven with our everyday lives in the here and now? Because we are looking forward to the Lord's return and our future home in Heaven, we are to live righteous lives, at peace with God.

C. S. Lewis, in *Mere Christianity*, makes the case that our hope of Heaven is the greatest motivator for living boldly for

Christ in this earthly life. He writes, "A continual looking forward to the eternal world is not (as some modern people think) a form of escapism or wishful thinking, but one of the things a Christian is meant to do. . . . If you read history you will find that the Christians who did most for the present world were just those who thought most of the next. The Apostles themselves, who set on foot the conversion of the Roman Empire, the great men who built up the Middle Ages, the English Evangelicals who abolished the Slave Trade, all left their mark on Earth precisely because their minds were occupied with Heaven."[3]

One of the great tragedies of the church today is that so many preachers neglect to preach about Heaven. They preach on every other conceivable subject—relationships and social issues and how to live effectively in *this* life—but they scarcely mention the joys that await us in Heaven. But if you want to be an effective Christian in *this* life, you must keep your expectations focused on the *next* life. Think about Heaven, focus on Heaven, and look forward to Heaven.

The First Heaven

Christians are often surprised when I tell them that the Bible speaks of three Heavens. We tend to think of just one Heaven, but according to God's Word, there are three.

People are even more surprised when I tell them what the first Heaven is. It's not where God is. The first Heaven is actually the devil's domain. It's where Satan and his demons reside. Paul refers to this first Heaven in Ephesians 6:12:

"Our struggle is not against flesh and blood, but against the rulers, against the authorities, against the powers of this dark world and against the spiritual forces of evil in the heavenly realms."

The first Heaven is the heavenly realm where Satan dwells and has authority. It is important for every believer to understand that we Christians play a profoundly important role in God's plan for the universe. In Ephesians 3:10, Paul explains God's intentions: "Now, through the church, the manifold wisdom of God should be made known to the rulers and authorities in the heavenly realms."

That is a truth that should transform your life. It's one of my most rock-solid anchors. Paul tells us that our faithfulness to God demonstrates to Satan and all of his demons that God is true and right, and that his judgment against Satan is righteous and just. When you focus on this biblical truth, you will never again take for granted your faithfulness to God. You will never again think it doesn't really matter whether you obey God or not. You are Exhibit A before Satan and his fallen angels, and your faithfulness proves God right—and it proves the demons wrong.

Where is the first Heaven located? It's right here, on Earth. We live in the first Heaven. It includes the visible domain all around us and the unseen realm where a battle is raging between God's angels and the demons of Satan.

In Daniel 10, an angel appears to Daniel and speaks of the invisible war and the opposition he faced from "the prince of Persia" and "the prince of Greece"—opposition so strong that this angel needed help from the archangel Michael, Israel's angelic prince, in order to prevail. In the first Heaven, angels and demons have authority over the nations and kingdoms of the earth. A battle is raging around us that we cannot see or hear, but it has enormous influence over our lives and the events in our world.

As I look around at the destruction of lives and the decline of our civilization and moral order, I can't help but conclude that demonic forces have been unleashed on our society. If you want to understand the explosion of drug addiction and violent crime, and the destructive ideologies spouted by supposedly educated (i.e., indoctrinated) people—remember the invisible war in the first Heaven.

Why are children being exposed to soul-destroying explicit pornography in public schools?[4] Why are school children being indoctrinated in "queer theory" and being made to question their God-given sexual identity? Why are parents deprived of the right to be informed that their children are being pushed into gender confusion by teachers and counselors?[5] Why are government officials claiming that school children belong to the public schools and the state, not to their parents?[6]

All this, I am convinced, is collateral damage from the invisible war in the first Heaven.

We cannot *see* the warfare in the first Heaven, but as believers we are all combatants in that war. We play our part in the invisible war through our obedience to God's Word, through our faithfulness to Jesus Christ, through sharing the good news of salvation with others, and through constant, daily, even hourly prayer.

The Second Heaven

The Bible speaks of the second Heaven, the universe of the celestial Heaven. Psalm 19 opens with these words: "The heavens declare the glory of God; the skies proclaim the work of his hands. Day after day they pour forth speech; night after night they reveal knowledge" (Psalm 19:1-2).

When you look up at the sky at night or you view a photo taken by an orbiting space telescope, you are looking at the second Heaven. This is the Heaven that inspired the great Christian hymn "How Great Thou Art."

In 1885, a Swedish poet named Carl Boberg was walking home after attending an afternoon church service in Kronobäck, Sweden. As he walked, he listened to the ringing of church bells. While the bells were ringing, a thundercloud darkened the sky, lightning flashed, and thunder shook the air. A wind blew up, followed by cool rain. Within minutes, the storm blew past, and a rainbow appeared.

By the time Boberg reached the front door of his house, he could see that the nearby Bay of Mönsterås was as still and reflective as a mirror. It was as if the storm and winds had never happened. Boberg was awed by the power of God on dramatic display in nature—with wind, rain, and lightning appearing suddenly and dramatically, then vanishing without a trace in minutes. He sat down at his desk and began to write the hymn he titled "O Store Gud."[7]

In 1949, English missionary Stuart K. Hine composed an English translation of the song, along with several additional verses. The English title was "How Great Thou Art." The song was later popularized by Cliff Barrows and George Beverly Shea during the Billy Graham evangelistic crusades.

"How Great Thou Art" was inspired by the spectacle of lightning, thunder, and wind that Carl Boberg witnessed. It was also inspired by the stars and the worlds that were hung in space by the hand of God. When Carl Boberg and Stuart K. Hine wrote of God's mighty power throughout the universe on display, they were writing about the second Heaven.

The stars in the second Heaven are God's oldest testament. They are God's silent preachers who never tire of proclaiming God's glory, by day and by night. They testify that our God is a mighty God, that our God is a God of miracles, that our God is the Lord not only of our planet, but of the entire universe.

Long before there were prophets, priests, apostles, or evangelists, before the Word of God was written down, the stars proclaimed the glory of God. His power, presence, and personality are declared in the second Heaven.

God made human beings with the ability to walk upright. Most animals walk on four or more legs or slither on their bellies. Why do human beings walk upright? I'm convinced that it's because God, when he created human beings in his own image, wanted men and women to be able to look up and to see the glory of the second Heaven.

I'm often asked, "If people need to believe in Jesus and be

born again to be saved, what about all the people who haven't heard about Jesus?" I reply, "The answer to your question is in Romans 1:20: 'For since the creation of the world God's invisible qualities—his eternal power and divine nature—have been clearly seen, being understood from what has been made, so that people are without excuse.'"

Paul says that God's silent preachers in the second Heaven speak so loudly and clearly of the glory of God that the gospel is written in the stars. Those who refuse and reject God are without excuse. All they have to do is look up at the stars and realize that God put them there. The stars and planets and galaxies are God's handiwork.

The renowned American minister and author Henry Ward Beecher owned a beautiful globe. It didn't depict the earth. Instead, it depicted the night sky, showing the positions of all the stars and constellations of the second Heaven. One day, writer and speaker Robert Ingersoll, who was known as the Great Agnostic, visited Beecher at his home. Ingersoll admired the celestial globe, and he asked Beecher who made it.

"Why, nobody made it," Beecher replied with a grin. "It just happened."[8]

Beecher was making the same point the apostle Paul makes in Romans 1:20: Anyone who rejects God after beholding the glories and wonders of his second Heaven is without excuse. The heavens declare the glory of God. The heavens can't *contain* his glory, because he is infinitely wise, loving, powerful, and creative. But the heavens *declare* his glory.

It is time—in fact, the time has long since passed—when believers should no longer be intimidated by doubters, agnostics, and skeptics. Tell them to look at the stars, for the stars declare the glory of God. If they can reject God after witnessing the wonders of the night sky, then their argument is not with us but with the universe itself. They are denying what is written plainly all across the second Heaven.

The Third Heaven

Next, we come to the third Heaven. It is the place the Scriptures call Paradise. This is the place Jesus spoke of on the cross when he promised the repentant thief, "Truly I tell you, today you will be with me in paradise" (Luke 23:43).

The apostle Paul tells us he saw Paradise, the third Heaven, with his own eyes. There he saw and heard things he was not permitted to disclose. If I had such an experience, I don't think I could obey the heavenly gag order. I would explode if I couldn't tell everyone what I had seen and heard in the third Heaven. And I think that, between the lines, you can hear a touch of frustration in Paul's words that he is forbidden to talk about the indescribable wonders of Paradise.

The third Heaven is where all Christian believers go when they die. If you have loved ones who have died as believers, that is where they are right now.

But Paradise, the third Heaven, is not the *New* Heaven that Jesus promised us. When the New Heaven comes, the old Heaven will be rolled away. Revelation 21:1 tells us, "Then I saw 'a new heaven and a new earth,' for the first heaven and the first earth had passed away, and there was no longer any sea."

Many Christians are surprised to learn that God is going to replace the present Heaven and earth with a New Heaven and a New Earth. But that is exactly what God's Word promises.

About 71 percent of the earth's surface is covered with water. There is also water vapor in the air, moisture in the soil, and water in plants, animals, and human bodies. Scientists have been eagerly searching for evidence of water on the moon and Mars, because in order to establish human bases on those worlds, they will need to find water to support life.

But in the New Heaven and New Earth, we won't need water. We will have glorified resurrection bodies. The third Heaven, or Paradise—though it is full of indescribable wonders according to Paul—is not even close to being as wonderful as the New Heaven that will come into existence when Jesus returns.

The third Heaven is where our Lord Jesus Christ is right now. He is our great High Priest, and he is constantly interceding for us with the Father. That's why he wants us to pray, "Our Father in heaven." Whenever you speak those words, you recognize the reality of Heaven, where Jesus intercedes on our behalf. As Paul tells us, "There is one God and one mediator between God and mankind, the man Christ Jesus" (1 Timothy 2:5). And, as the book of Hebrews reminds us,

"Therefore he is able to save completely those who come to God through him, because he always lives to intercede for them" (Hebrews 7:25).

Jesus was interceding for you and me even before he was crucified, and he still intercedes for us today. In his high priestly prayer, in John 17, Jesus pulls back the curtain and shows us how he is continually interceding for us. Just hours before his crucifixion, Jesus prays to the Father, "My prayer is not for them [the disciples] alone. I pray also for those who will believe in me through their message" (John 17:20). Jesus prays for all believers in all places at all times—and that includes you and me.

Jesus alone is our great High Priest—not his mother, Mary, and not the saints. The Catholic Church encourages its adherents to pray to a vast pantheon of saints, but there is no biblical support for this practice. In fact, the Bible says there is only one mediator between God and humanity: Jesus alone. So, though we honor and respect Mary, we do not pray to her. She cannot help us. Instead, we pray to her son, Jesus, the Son of God, who intercedes on our behalf with God the Father. He alone is our High Priest.

It is thrilling beyond measure to know that Jesus intercedes for us. On the cross, he gave his life for us. Now, in the third Heaven, he intercedes for us and prays for us.

The third Heaven is the Heaven where God's perspective reigns supreme. The third Heaven looks down on the second and first Heavens. God the Father looks down from the highest Heaven. He looks down on that ancient serpent, Satan, and he says, "Don't forget, Satan, that I am in charge of every level of Heaven. You were defeated at the cross. Your throne is my footstool. Your days on earth are numbered. You can only roam the earth for a limited time. Soon I will bind you with chains and throw you into the abyss of Hell."[9]

Tragically, many human souls will end up in the abyss with Satan. You and I need to do everything in our power to keep people out of Hell and point them to Heaven instead. Are you winning souls for the Lord Jesus Christ? Are you making Jesus known to your friends? Have you told them about the miracle that God is working in your life and how he has saved you from death and Hell?

In the Old Testament book of Daniel, we read this astounding statement: "Those who are wise will shine like the brightness of the heavens, and those who lead many to righteousness, like the stars for ever and ever" (Daniel 12:3). And in Proverbs, we read, "One who is wise gains souls" (Proverbs 11:30, NASB).

Are you wise, as defined by God's Word? Are you winning lost souls for Jesus? If you are gaining souls for God's Kingdom, you will shine like the stars for all eternity. That is God's promise to you.

There may be some who are reading this book who are a little worried—maybe even scared—because I have written about the reality of Hell and the seriousness of making sure we are going to Heaven. If you feel a tug of fear right now, that's good. I call that a "sanctified scare." If you have not settled the matter of your eternal destiny, then you *should* be scared. But you don't have to fear Hell any longer.

You can know that your eternal destiny is settled. You can know that you are going to Paradise, the third Heaven, when you die—and you will have a place reserved for you in the New Heaven when Jesus returns. Go to God in prayer right now. Confess that you are a sinner. Repent of your sins. Ask Jesus to save you and to take control of your life. Do that, and even if you die today, you'll have the same assurance that Jesus gave to the thief on the cross: "Today you will be with me in paradise" (Luke 23:43).

7

A NEW HEAVEN
AND A NEW EARTH

CAN YOU NAME THE FOUR CHAPTERS in the Bible where Satan and his works are completely absent? They are the first two chapters in the book of Genesis and the last two chapters in the book of Revelation. Satan makes his first appearance in Genesis 3. He is busy opposing God and harassing humanity throughout the Bible until Revelation 20, when God casts him into the lake of fire. So the first two chapters of Genesis and the last two chapters of Revelation are the only chapters in which there is no satanic influence.

The devil hates the entire Bible. But he has a special, seething hatred for Genesis and Revelation. He despises these two books more than anything else.

Satan hates Genesis because that is where God pronounces his death sentence. God addresses the devil (who has taken the form of a snake), and says, "I will put enmity between you and the woman, and between your offspring and hers; he will crush your head, and you will strike his heel" (Genesis 3:15). Satan struck the heel of Jesus at the Cross; but Jesus crushed Satan's head.

Satan hates Revelation because that is where God carries out the sentence of eternal punishment against him. John writes, "The devil, who deceived them, was thrown into the lake of burning sulfur, where the beast and the false prophet had been thrown. They will be tormented day and night for ever and ever" (Revelation 20:10).

How do we know that Satan has a special hatred for these two books of the Bible? We can see it in the campaigns of opposition and subversion carried out against Genesis and Revelation by Satan's human servants. Even in the evangelical church, there is no shortage of false preachers who claim that Genesis is a myth and Revelation an impenetrable mystery. They try to persuade Christians to ignore and disbelieve both books. Satan, the father of lies, is behind all of these attacks on the validity of Genesis and Revelation.

Satan wants us to doubt God's Word, and he especially wants to undermine the credibility of Genesis and Revelation. But God's Word is the absolute truth. Our Lord is honored when his children not only read and heed the Word, but obey and live by it.

Passing Away

The Word of God is amazingly consistent. We can clearly see the consistency of God's Word in regard to the prophecy of a New Heaven and a New Earth.

Seven hundred years before the time of Christ, the prophet Isaiah wrote, "See, I will create new heavens and a new earth. The former things will not be remembered, nor will they come to mind" (Isaiah 65:17).

The Lord Jesus Christ says, "Heaven and earth will pass away, but my words will never pass away" (Matthew 24:35; Mark 13:31; Luke 21:33).

And the apostle Peter, in his second epistle, writes, "By the same word the present heavens and earth are reserved for fire, being kept for the day of judgment and destruction of the ungodly. . . . But in keeping with his promise we are looking forward to a new heaven and a new earth, where righteousness dwells" (2 Peter 3:7, 13).

The Word of God is consistent. The Word of God is absolutely true. Among my favorite portions of Scripture are those that speak of the joy of believers in Heaven, the New Jerusalem. When we read the last two chapters of the book of Revelation, we find that everything is brand new.

God is going to swing his cosmic wrecking ball at the old universe. He will destroy sin, Satan, and all the false religious and political systems that have oppressed humanity since the Fall. He will bring into existence a New Heaven and a New Earth—and the capital city at the center of his new creation will be the New Jerusalem.

Revelation 21 begins, "Then I saw 'a new heaven and a new earth,' for the first heaven and the first earth had passed away, and there was no longer any sea. I saw the Holy City, the new Jerusalem, coming down out of heaven from God, prepared as a bride beautifully dressed for her husband" (Revelation 21:1-2). The translators placed the phrase "a new heaven and a new earth" in quotation marks because it appears to be a reference to Isaiah 65:17.

Imagine John's emotions as he beheld this vision from God—a vision of God's plan for the future of Heaven and Earth. John saw the Holy City, the New Jerusalem, descending from orbit and settling onto the New Earth. John tries to describe the dazzling beauty of the new city by comparing it to a beautifully arrayed bride. But words are inadequate to fully convey this truly stunning vision.

John goes on to say that he heard a loud voice declare, "God's dwelling place is now among the people, and he will dwell with them. They will be his people, and God himself will be with them and be their God" (Revelation 21:3).

The most important thing you should know about the New Jerusalem is that there will be nothing there to separate us from Jesus. There will be no sin, no disobedience. There will be no sorrows, no tears. There will be no heartbreaking divisions between brothers and sisters in Christ. God himself will be with us. We are going to be *with* Jesus and we are going to be *like* Jesus—because we are going to see him face-to-face. Can you imagine that?

The voice John hears goes on to say, "'He will wipe every

tear from their eyes. There will be no more death' or mourning or crying or pain, for the old order of things has passed away" (Revelation 21:4). This statement contains a quotation from Isaiah 25:8: "He will swallow up death forever. The Sovereign LORD will wipe away the tears from all faces."

Jesus will wipe away our tears. In the original language, the text literally says that he is going to wipe away *every last* tear. Sorrow will vanish from the universe and will never return.

The Alpha and the Omega

We tend to think of the word *no* as a negative. But what could be more blessed and positive than to be in a place where there is *no* separation, *no* death, *no* mourning, *no* crying, and *no* pain. In the New Jerusalem, there will be no cancer, no diabetes, no pandemics, no viruses, no bacterial infections. In the New Jerusalem, there will be no broken homes, no broken hearts, no child abuse, no domestic violence, no conflict, no loneliness, no tragedy of any kind. In the New Jerusalem, there will be no hospitals and no funeral homes.

Why? Because Jesus is there.

John writes, "He who was seated on the throne said, 'I am making everything new!' Then he said, 'Write this down, for these words are trustworthy and true.' He said to me: 'It is done. I am the Alpha and the Omega, the Beginning and the End. To the thirsty I will give water without cost from the spring of the water of life'" (Revelation 21:5-6).

Jesus is there and he directs John to write down his words

because they are a trustworthy and true revelation of God. Jesus calls himself the Alpha and the Omega, the First and the Last. He is saying, in effect, "I was there at the beginning of time and space, and I will be there when it all comes to an end. I am living water for a thirsty soul. I am the only one who can truly satisfy you. I am the only one who can make sense out of your senseless life. I am the only one who can give you victory. I am the only one who can make you a child of the living God."

Then Jesus, speaking through John, tells us who will—and who will not—be in Heaven: "Those who are victorious will inherit all this, and I will be their God and they will be my children. But the cowardly, the unbelieving, the vile, the murderers, the sexually immoral, those who practice magic arts, the idolaters and all liars—they will be consigned to the fiery lake of burning sulfur. This is the second death'" (Revelation 21:7-8).

Those who abuse and twist and deny God's Word will not be there. In fact, Paul records a similar list in two of his letters, 1 Corinthians and Galatians:

"Or do you not know that wrongdoers will not inherit the kingdom of God? Do not be deceived: Neither the sexually immoral nor idolaters nor adulterers nor men who have sex with men nor thieves nor the greedy nor drunkards nor slanderers nor swindlers will inherit the kingdom of God" (1 Corinthians 6:9-10).

"The acts of the flesh are obvious: sexual immorality, impurity and debauchery; idolatry and witchcraft; hatred, discord, jealousy, fits of rage, selfish ambition, dissensions, factions and envy; drunkenness, orgies, and the like. I warn you, as I did before, that those who live like this will not inherit the kingdom of God" (Galatians 5:19-21).

These are passages of God's Word that we dare not take lightly. God always says what he means and means what he says.

The New Jerusalem

Over the past two decades, there has been a glut of books by people who claim to have died and visited Heaven, and then were medically revived and brought back to their earthly lives. Why do publishers keep selling these books? The answer is simple: People keep buying them. Some of these titles have remained on the bestseller lists for several years—in fact, they have their own genre: "Heaven tourism" books.

Enough of these books have been published that you have to wonder why God would allow so many temporary visitors into Heaven. Who would have thought that Heaven would be such a popular tourist destination? But no one gets a tourist visa to Heaven. God doesn't make mistakes. He doesn't accidentally let people crash the gates of Heaven, then throw them back into their pain-wracked earthly bodies. How do I know? Because the Bible says, "People are destined to die once, and after that to face judgment" (Hebrews 9:27). When a believer dies, he or she goes to Paradise—but no one is allowed in early.

In the biblical account, the martyr Stephen got a glimpse

of Heaven shortly before his death. The apostle Paul was swept up into the third Heaven, but he was forbidden to even mention what he saw and heard—much less write a book about it. John saw Heaven in a vision and recorded his majestic description in Revelation. God gave these three men special glimpses of Heaven for special reasons at a special time in history. But certainly he isn't operating a tour bus to Heaven in the twenty-first century.

If you want to know what Heaven is really like, there's only one bestseller you need—and that's the Bible. Everything you need to know about Heaven and how to get there is in the Bible. Anything anyone writes about Heaven that is not found in the Bible is not to be trusted.

And here's something else to think about: Let's suppose that one of those "Heaven tourism" books turned out to be true. Let's suppose that someone really did nearly die, was transported to Heaven for a brief time, and then returned to tell about it. Where did that person go? Not to the New Heaven that the Bible promises will one day be our eternal home. No, that person would only have visited Paradise. I'm sure Paradise is wonderful, but I also know that Paradise doesn't begin to compare with the New Heaven that God has promised us in his Word.

Hebrews 11:10 tells us that, by faith in God, Abraham "was looking forward to the city with foundations, whose architect and builder is God." What was the city Abraham was waiting for? It was the Holy City, the New Jerusalem, the capital of the New Heaven.

Cain, the firstborn son of Adam, who murdered his brother Abel, founded the first city ever built (see Genesis 4:17). But the city Cain built was an ungodly city. The Babylonians began building the first skyscraper, the tower of Babel, but it was an ungodly project. The city that the Lord God designed is the heavenly city, the Holy City, the New Jerusalem.

Hebrews refers to the New Jerusalem as "Mount Zion . . . the city of the living God, the heavenly Jerusalem," where there will be "thousands upon thousands of angels in joyful assembly" (Hebrews 12:22). Here on Earth, you may live in a great city. You may even live in the *old* Jerusalem, the capital of modern Israel; but Hebrews reminds us that "For we do not have an enduring city, but we are looking for the city that is to come" (Hebrews 13:14).

Earthly Jerusalem used to be a holy city. Today, however, Jerusalem is a blood-stained city. It is stained with the blood of the Savior, the Messiah, the Lord whom God sent. The earthly Jerusalem rejected and crucified the Anointed One of God. Jesus didn't redeem us so that we could live in an earthly Jerusalem, a piece of real estate in the Middle East. He redeemed us to live forever in the New Jerusalem.

Billions of Mansions

What will this Holy City, the New Jerusalem, be like?

The apostle John describes how an angel said to him, "Come, I will show you the bride, the wife of the Lamb" (Revelation 21:9). Then the angel carried John to a high mountaintop and showed him "the Holy City, Jerusalem, coming down out of heaven from God" (Revelation 21:10).

The city "shone with the glory of God, and its brilliance was like that of a very precious jewel" (Revelation 21:11). The city was surrounded by a high wall with twelve gates, and an angel guarded each gate. On those gates were inscribed the names of the twelve tribes of Israel. The city wall was built on twelve foundations, and on each foundation was inscribed the name of one of the twelve apostles of Jesus (Revelation 21:12-14).

The twelve gates represent the Old Testament believers. The twelve foundations represent the New Testament apostles, who laid the gospel foundation of the church. Those who deny the truth of the Word of God, both the Old and New Testaments, will not be in that city. They will not pass through its gates nor stand on its foundation, because they have rejected the teaching of God's Word.

Revelation 21:16 tells us, "The city was laid out like a square, as long as it was wide." The angel who showed John the New Jerusalem "measured the city with the rod and found it to be 12,000 stadia in length, and as wide and high as it is long." You may wonder what "stadia" are. Bible scholars have converted stadia to miles and have done the math. The size of the New Jerusalem is nothing short of incredible: 1,400 miles high, 1,400 miles wide, and 1,400 miles long.

To what can we compare these dimensions? The 12,000-stadia length of the New Jerusalem is *greater* than the driving distance from Atlanta to Denver, or from Los Angeles to

Kansas City, or from Miami to Boston. The volume of the New Jerusalem is nearly 2.75 *billion* cubic miles.

Dr. Henry Morris made a rough calculation of the population density of the New Jerusalem. He started with an assumption that there have been 100 billion people born throughout history and that 20 percent were saved. The result is that the Holy City would need room for 20 billion people. How densely packed would those people be? Based on the size of the New Jerusalem as described by John, every single believer could have a cube-shaped block of the city to call his or her own—and each block would measure seventy-five acres per side.[1]

No wonder Jesus said, "In my Father's house are many mansions" (John 14:2, KJV). A cubical structure that is 1,400 miles high, 1,400 miles long, and 1,400 miles wide certainly has enough space for billions of mansions.

The New Jerusalem is described in brilliant imagery. It is a structure made of shining, multicolored jasper, sapphire, agate, emerald, onyx, ruby, chrysolite, beryl, topaz, turquoise, jacinth, amethyst, pearl, and the purest gold. The precious gems and metals that we prize so highly in this life will be mere construction materials, like brick and concrete, in the life to come.

Where Is the Temple?

Next, John makes an interesting observation. He looks around, expecting to see a great house of worship—but there is none. Then he realizes why: "I did not see a temple in the city, because the Lord God Almighty and the Lamb are its temple" (Revelation 21:22).

In Old Testament times, God told Moses to build a Tabernacle and he told Solomon to build the magnificent Temple in Jerusalem. God commanded the construction of physical structures as symbols of his presence with his people. Those physical structures were symbolic pictures of God's future dwelling place among his people—the dwelling place described in Revelation 21. But when the real thing comes, we won't need the picture.

If you are away from your loved ones, you may often pause to gaze at their photos on your smartphone. But once you and your loved one are together in the same room, you don't need to look at the photos. The real McCoy, your beloved family, is right there with you, close enough to talk to and embrace. That's how it will be when God dwells among his people in the New Jerusalem. We won't need a Temple because we will *be* God's Temple.

There will be no need for the sun or the moon, and there will be no night, because God's light will illuminate the Holy City. The nations will be guided by that light.

In Revelation 21:25, John writes, "On no day will its gates ever be shut." Later he adds, "Nothing impure will ever enter it, nor will anyone who does what is shameful or deceitful, but only those whose names are written in the Lamb's book of life" (Revelation 21:27). You might wonder: How will God keep impure, deceitful people out of the New Jerusalem if its gates are never shut?

The answer is found in Revelation 21:8, where Jesus says to John that all those who engage in immorality, deception, and vile practices will be "consigned to the fiery lake . . . the second death." The gates of the New Jerusalem will remain open at all times, because only those whose names are written in the Book of Life will be in that city.

The citizens of the New Jerusalem will be sinners who are saved by grace. Because Jesus died as a sacrifice for their sins, they are no longer impure. Their sins are covered by the blood of Jesus, who was crucified for them. They have received the gift of his pure righteousness by grace through faith. They will walk in that city and they will celebrate in that city.

The River of Life

Next, John describes the River of Life: "The angel showed me the river of the water of life, as clear as crystal, flowing from the throne of God and of the Lamb down the middle of the great street of the city" (Revelation 22:1-2). It won't be like any earthly river. The River of Life will flow with indescribable, inexhaustible blessings.

Robert Lowry was a nineteenth-century Baptist preacher and songwriter whose hymns and gospel songs include "Christ Arose!," "How Can I Keep from Singing?," and "Nothing but the Blood of Jesus." These are songs we don't hear very much anymore, and I think that's a tragedy, because Lowry's music is rich in biblical truth.

What is perhaps his most famous song, "Shall We Gather

at the River?" is one I used to sing in church as a boy. The lyrics capture Robert Lowry's interpretation of John's vision in Revelation 22. The song begins:

Shall we gather at the river,
Where bright angel feet have trod;
With its crystal tide forever
Flowing by the throne of God?

The chorus answers the question posed by the verse:

Yes, we'll gather at the river,
The beautiful, the beautiful river;
Gather with the saints at the river
That flows by the throne of God.[2]

The crystal tide of the River of Life flows from the throne of God. You and I and the rest of the great throng of believers will gather around the throne, around that River of Life, to worship the Lord and celebrate his gift of eternal life. There will be no night there because God himself is the Light of Heaven. With its beauty and variety and crystalline purity, the River of Life will be a fountain of unending blessing and eternal life with Christ.

What is the "throne of God" that John speaks of? He is not describing a piece of furniture for a person to sit on. The throne of God is nothing less than the fixed center of the universe. It's the immovable point of reference for all of time and space. It is the hub around which the entire universe revolves.

The River of Life flows from God's throne, from the fixed center of all of his creation.

The Tree of Life

John goes on to describe a special tree in the New Jerusalem: "On each side of the river stood the tree of life, bearing twelve crops of fruit, yielding its fruit every month. And the leaves of the tree are for the healing of the nations" (Revelation 22:2).

The first mention in Scripture of the tree of life is in Genesis 2:9: "The LORD God made all kinds of trees grow out of the ground—trees that were pleasing to the eye and good for food. In the middle of the garden were the tree of life and the tree of the knowledge of good and evil."

In the Garden of Eden, God told Adam and Eve they could eat the fruit of every tree in the Garden but one— the tree of the knowledge of good and evil. Satan tempted Adam and Eve, and they ate from the forbidden tree—and sin entered the spiritual DNA of the human race.

After the Fall, God sent Adam and Eve out of the Garden of Eden, and he placed angels and a flaming sword to keep sinful humanity away from the tree of life. Through Adam's disobedience, we all (as Adam's descendants) became depraved and sinful, incapable of living a righteous life. Adam's sin brought not only spiritual death but physical death as well. That's why nobody can live forever on this earth.

But we will live forever in the New Jerusalem. We will gather around the tree of life, the symbol of everlasting life in Heaven with God.

Is the tree of life in Revelation the same tree that we read about in Genesis? Yes, God's Word says that this same tree of life that once stood in the Garden of Eden is now in Paradise: "Whoever has ears, let them hear what the Spirit says to the churches. To the one who is victorious, I will give the right to eat from the tree of life, which is in the paradise of God" (Revelation 2:7).

When the New Jerusalem comes to rest on the New Earth, the tree of life will be there, planted in such a way that it stands astride both banks of the River of Life. It will produce "twelve crops of fruit, yielding its fruit every month," and its leaves will be "for the healing of the nations" (Revelation 22:1-2). The tree speaks of the abundance of Heaven as well as the life-giving and healing powers of Heaven.

Notice the fascinating statement that the leaves of the tree of life are for the healing of the nations. Why do the nations need to be healed? They need healing from their inclination to disobey, reject, and rebel against God. As King David observed: "Why do the nations conspire and the peoples plot in vain? The kings of the earth rise up and the rulers band together against the LORD and against his anointed" (Psalm 2:1-2).

In the New Jerusalem, not only individual believers but

entire nations will be healed of their rebelliousness by the life-giving leaves of the tree of life. The nations will be reconciled to their Creator. The Revelation account of the tree of life echoes the Garden of Eden account and points our hearts to our future hope in Heaven.

No More Curse

John goes on to write, "No longer will there be any curse. The throne of God and of the Lamb will be in the city, and his servants will serve him. They will see his face, and his name will be on their foreheads" (Revelation 22:3-4).

This is a profound and inspiring statement. No more curse! All our lives, we have been living in a world cursed by sin. In the New Jerusalem, there will no longer be any curse. God's throne will be the center and focus of the city. We, God's servants, will serve him and we will see him face-to-face.

This is an amazing truth. Nobody has ever seen the face of God. Even Moses, who was God's servant and who ascended the holy mountain to receive the tablets of the Law from God, never saw God's face. But you and I will see the face of God in Heaven, in the place where there is no more curse of sin.

Instead we will see God face-to-face, and his name will be on our foreheads, says John in Revelation 22:4.

I once preached about the coming Antichrist and how millions of people would be cursed by accepting his mark, "the mark of the beast," on their foreheads. I later learned that a precious twelve-year-old girl in our congregation heard that message and took it very seriously. She went home and wrote the name of Jesus on her forehead with a washable marker. When her parents asked her why, she said, "Because I don't want the Antichrist to have his name on my forehead."

She made sure that there would be no room on her forehead for the mark of the beast. She had stamped the name of Jesus on her face and on her soul. In the New Heaven, we will all have the name of God stamped on our foreheads.

On October 12, 1900, there was a wedding in London, England. The bridegroom's name was William Montague Dyke, the son of a prominent member of Parliament. He was engaged to the daughter of Admiral John Halliday Cave, a well-known retired Royal Navy officer.

What makes this story extraordinary is one surprising fact: William Dyke had never seen the face of his bride-to-be. Though they had spent countless hours together, talking and getting to know each other, Mr. Dyke didn't know what Miss Cave looked like—for one simple reason: William Dyke was blind.

At the age of ten, he had suffered an accident that cost him his sight in both eyes. He worked hard at his studies and graduated from Cambridge University with honors. At a social gathering, he met Miss Cave. He fell in love with her voice, her touch, her mind, and her compassionate spirit. And she fell in love with him.

During the time they were discussing marriage, William Dyke went to one of England's most prominent eye surgeons and asked if there were any way his sight might be restored—even if only for an hour. It turned out there was an experimental surgery that could be tried, and the surgeon agreed to perform the operation.

Young Mr. Dyke had just one condition. He wanted the bandages to be removed on the day of the wedding while he was standing at the altar. He wanted the first vision he saw to be the face of his beloved bride.

So, on the appointed day, Mr. Dyke stood at the church altar. Standing next to him, in the place of the best man, was the eye surgeon.

The organist played the "Wedding March," the doctor cut and removed the bandages from Mr. Dyke's eyes, and the bride made her way down the aisle. The people in the audience held their breath until the bridegroom said, "At last! At last!" as he gazed upon the face of his bride.[3]

You and I have never seen God's face. In a similar way, it's as if we've spent our entire lives on earth in total blindness, unable to see the face of the one we worship. When we see him for the first time, I believe our faces will shine with the reflected light of our Lord, our God, our Savior. And we will cry out, "At last! At last!"

As 1 John 3:2 promises: "We know that when Christ appears, we shall be like him, for we shall see him as he is." Are you ready for that day?

"Lord, Save Me!"

Revelation 22:6 is the last verse of the prophetic message of Revelation: "The angel said to me, 'These words are trustworthy and true. The Lord, the God who inspires the prophets, sent his angel to show his servants the things that must soon take place.'"

All the prophetic events foretold in the book of Revelation will take place as written. They will be fulfilled. What is now prophecy will one day become history. Just as all the Old Testament prophecies of the coming of Jesus into the world were fulfilled in exacting detail, so too the prophecies of his return and the revelation of a New Heaven, a New Earth, and the New Jerusalem will come to pass.

In Revelation 22:11, Jesus makes a statement that seems baffling to our ears: "Let the one who does wrong continue to do wrong; let the vile person continue to be vile; let the one who does right continue to do right; and let the holy person continue to be holy." You would expect him to call the wrongdoers and the vile people to repent; but instead he says, let them continue to sin. Why? What does he mean?

Our Lord wants us to know that once our earthly life is over, the die has been cast. The decisions we make in this life affect eternity. Will we spend eternity in Heaven with Jesus— or in the lake of fire with Satan? Once you have passed from this life into eternity, there is no second chance.

False preachers and false teachers will tell you that God will let everyone into Heaven, no matter how they have lived in this life. But you won't find any such teaching in the Word of God. There is no opportunity to repent after you die. Those who die in the state of unbelief will remain in that state of unbelief until the Day of Judgment. It gives me no joy to say that—but it gives me a sense of urgency.

Luke 23 records that two criminals were crucified on either side of the cross of Jesus. One of them reviled Jesus and insulted him. The other said, "Jesus, remember me when you come into your kingdom" (Luke 23:42). Those nine words made all the difference in that man's eternal destiny. Jesus replied, "Truly I tell you, today you will be with me in paradise" (Luke 23:43).

Knowing and trusting Jesus makes all the difference in eternity—and also in this life. Knowing Jesus makes all the difference in how we face temptation, in how we face trials and sufferings, in how we deal with stress and opposition, in how we experience the joys and triumphs of this life. When we know Jesus, our life in Heaven begins on earth.

The brief nine-word prayer of the criminal on the cross is a lengthy soliloquy compared to Peter's three-word plea for salvation. When Jesus walked on water and called, "Come," to Peter, the eager apostle climbed out of his fishing boat and began walking on the water toward Jesus—but his faith soon wavered and he cried out, "Lord, save me!" (see Matthew 14:29-31).

You can pray with Peter those three words, "Lord, save me!" And I urge you not to wait another moment before doing so. The Bible says, "Now is the time of God's favor, now is the day of salvation" (2 Corinthians 6:2). I plead with you: Settle the question of your eternity and the rest of your life right now, before another moment passes.

The Water of Life

I wish you could see my face as I write these words. I wish you could sense the intense emotions in my heart at this moment. I get choked up and teary-eyed when I think and write about this subject because I know what's at stake. I know the warnings and urgings and pleadings contained in the Word of God.

In Revelation 22:12, Jesus says, "Look, I am coming soon! My reward is with me, and I will give to each person according to what they have done." When Jesus returns, he will come to judge the entire human race. There will be a judgment for unbelievers, and there will also be a judgment for believers.

The judgment for believers will not be a judgment of condemnation. It will not be a judgment to determine whether they are saved or lost. They are already saved by grace through faith. Instead, it will be a judgment of *rewards*. Jesus tells us there will be a merit system in Heaven. We will be rewarded according to our faithfulness to the Lord. We will be rewarded according to how much we sacrificed to advance the Kingdom of God.

God is not a Marxist. He doesn't distribute the same reward to all people regardless of merit. No, God rewards each believer according to what they have done. There will be a reward system in Heaven, and it will not be *equal*—in other words, not everyone will get the same reward. No, but the reward system in Heaven will be *righteous* and *just*. Everyone will be rewarded according to what they have done in this earthly life.

In Revelation 22:17, we read, "The Spirit and the bride say, 'Come!' And let the one who hears say, 'Come!' Let the one who is thirsty come; and let the one who wishes take the free gift of the water of life." This is an invitation to unbelievers and believers alike.

Even as believers, we live in a spiritually parched culture. We easily fall into thinking and acting like the world around us, to the point where we become dry and parched and lifeless, even though we have access to the well of living water. We start to think the way the world thinks. We think that money and material things can satisfy us. Or that we would be happy if our political ideology prevailed. Or that life would be perfect if we could have a fat retirement portfolio or the perfect vacation or a different person at our side.

That is parched thinking. Those are satanic delusions. They are lies. Don't believe them.

Only Jesus can satisfy our longings.

Revelation 22:20 tells us, "He who testifies to these things says, 'Yes, I am coming soon.' Amen. Come, Lord Jesus."

This is a promise—*and* a warning. Jesus will return soon, and all believers await his coming with hope and eager expectation. At the same time, we know that everyone will have to face him. "At the name of Jesus every knee should bow, in heaven and on earth and under the earth" (Philippians 2:10). We will all, without exception, confess that Jesus is Lord—whether we confess him willingly and joyfully—or with fear and regret.

So let's search our hearts now, while there is still time. The time is coming—and coming soon—when there won't be any more chances. Are you in the faith? Are you living for Jesus? When the New Heaven and the New Earth are revealed, will you be there to enjoy its splendors throughout eternity?

8

ON EARTH
AS IT IS IN HEAVEN

A FARMER TOOK THE NEW country preacher to his property and stood with him on a small hill next to the homestead. Pointing north, the farmer said to the preacher, "As far as your eye can see in this direction, I own." Turning to the west, he said, "As far as your eye can see in that direction, I own." Then he repeated his statement looking to the south and the east.

The preacher looked the farmer in the eye and said, "Let me ask you this." He pointed heavenward. "How much do you own in that direction?"

You may wonder, "Will we own things in Heaven?" You'd better believe we will! As the apostle Paul told Timothy, by doing good to others and sharing generously with others, Christians "will lay up treasure for themselves as a firm foundation for the coming age, so that they may take hold of the life that is truly life" (1 Timothy 6:19).[1]

We tend to focus on our finances, our investment portfolios, and our retirement plans. But Jesus said, "Store up for yourselves treasures in heaven, where moths and vermin do not destroy, and where thieves do not break in and steal" (Matthew 6:20).

Many people assume that the present life is real and concrete, and they can safely put off thinking about Heaven until later. The Bible tells us it's the other way around. Life on earth is slipping by and fading away. What is real and concrete is what we have invested in our heavenly home.

As believers, we have a heavenly savings plan. How much we invest *now* determines how much we will get back *later* in eternal rewards.

So look heavenward and ask yourself: "How much do I own in *that* direction? How much treasure am I laying up in Heaven? How much of a firm foundation am I building for eternity?"

Blessings in the Heavenly Realms

For a long time, I enjoyed 20/20 vision in both eyes. I was certain I would never need reading glasses. Then one morning when I was in my late forties, I took my Bible to the place where I have my morning devotions, and I opened it to begin reading—but I had trouble making out the words on the page.

Of course, the problem had to be that my reading lamp wasn't working. It was a three-way lamp and I had it on the highest, brightest setting, yet the light wasn't bright enough for me to focus on the words. I tried a new bulb, and still I had trouble reading the page. I turned on the ceiling lights. That didn't help either.

The previous day, I had read my Bible effortlessly. But that morning, I couldn't. Surely, my eyesight couldn't change that radically overnight!

And then it occurred to me: What if something was wrong with my eyes? What if I had been struck by some eye disease?

I called an eye doctor and said, "I need to come see you. I think I'm developing a problem with my eyesight."

He said, "Don't waste time coming to me. Go to the drugstore and buy some reading glasses—the lowest magnification they sell. That'll fix you right up."

"No, I don't need reading glasses! I have 20/20 vision."

"Trust me. Try the glasses."

That was hard for me to accept. But I went to the drugstore and bought a pair of reading glasses, and suddenly I was able to read again.

I realized that my lamp had not changed and the size of the type in my Bible had not changed. What had changed were the muscles in my eyes. They had weakened.

I discovered an important spiritual principle through that experience. We often find that the world seems out of focus and indecipherable. So we say, "If only I had more light! If only I had more power!" But we don't need more of either of those things. God has already given us all the light and power we need. We already possess every blessing we need.

Where are those blessings? In the heavenly realm. We just need to put on our biblical reading glasses so we can see them. How do we know we possess those blessings? Because Paul tells us we do: "Praise be to the God and Father of our Lord Jesus Christ, who has blessed us in the heavenly realms with every spiritual blessing in Christ" (Ephesians 1:3).

Paul goes on to tell the church in Ephesus that he has continually prayed for them, ever since he heard of their great faith in Christ. What did Paul ask God to give the Ephesian Christians? Did he ask God to give them more strength and power? *No.* More blessings? *No.* More faith? *No.* More joy? *No.* More love? *No.*

Here's what Paul said he prayed for: "I pray that the eyes of your heart may be enlightened in order that you may know the hope to which he has called you, the riches of his glorious inheritance in his holy people, and his incomparably great power for us who believe" (Ephesians 1:18-19). In short, Paul prayed that God would *open their eyes to see what God had already given them.*

God had already given the Ephesian believers all the strength, power, blessings, faith, joy, and love they needed. God had blessed them with every spiritual blessing in Christ in the heavenly realms. They already possessed it. Paul wanted them to *know* they possessed it.

Heaven in the Here and Now

Years ago, I was visiting with a friend from Texas, a business entrepreneur who had started or acquired a number of successful businesses. He said, "Michael, to tell you the truth, I have so many companies that I couldn't name them all. I really need to sit down with my advisors and have them help me get my arms around all that I own."

You and I are in the same situation. We possess so many spiritual blessings that we really don't know all that we possess. We can't name them all. We really need to get our arms around all the blessings that God has poured out on us from the heavenly realm.

Many Christians are familiar with these words of the apostle Paul: "'What no eye has seen, what no ear has heard, and what no human mind has conceived'—the things God has prepared for those who love him" (1 Corinthians 2:9). But we mistakenly think that Paul is only talking about what God has prepared for our future in Heaven. No, Paul is also talking about the here and now, as evidenced by the very next verse: "These are the things God has revealed to us by his Spirit" (1 Corinthians 2:10).

The Kingdom of Heaven is coming—but it is also already here. If we are walking with Jesus, if we live in his power according to his will, then we have his power in us. As Jesus said, "The coming of the kingdom of God is not something that can be observed, nor will people say, 'Here it is,' or 'There it is,' because the kingdom of God is in your midst"

(Luke 17:20-21). Or, as the King James Version translates it, "The kingdom of God is within you."

The blessings that God has *already* given us, and that he will *also* give us in the life to come, can never be understood by the natural mind. We need the Holy Spirit to help us comprehend all of the blessings that we have in Jesus.

Why is it important for you and me to grasp these incredible blessings from God? Because it is impossible for us to live a life of obedience until we comprehend who we are in Jesus Christ. Show me a professing Christian who is living in disobedience, and I'll show you a person who has not begun to grasp who they are in Jesus Christ.

When I was young and inclined to get into mischief, my parents would sit me down and tell me, "Remember who you are. Remember your family's name. Remember your family's reputation. Remember our Christian witness." They continually reminded me of who I was and the family and faith I represented. And the more I understood my identity as a follower of Christ, the less inclined I was to mischief and misdeeds.

If we would truly understand who we are in Christ and all the blessings we possess, it would change the way we live. It would change the decisions we make. It would change the way we respond to temptation. It would change our speech. It would radically energize our witness for Christ.

My prayer for you as you read these pages is that you would truly understand that Heaven is not merely about "the sweet by-and-by." It's about the here and now, as well. I pray that the Holy Spirit will open your eyes and reveal the blessings that God is pouring out on you—right here, right now. I pray that God would enable you to get your arms around all the blessings that he has given you from the heavenly realm.

The Dynamic Power of Heaven

Paul prayed that the Ephesians would understand God's "incomparably great power for us who believe" (Ephesians 1:19). He wanted them—and *all* believers—to know that God does not dispense his power to us in dribs and drabs. He has already made the full measure of his power available to those of us who believe. You cannot get any more of God's power than you already have. You have within you the awesome, dynamic power of Heaven.

What you need most is a full awareness of the power God has already given you. Only when you fully comprehend that dynamic power within you can you fully access it in a time of need.

Before Jesus ascended to Heaven, he said to his disciples, "You will receive power when the Holy Spirit comes on you; and you will be my witnesses in Jerusalem, and in all Judea and Samaria, and to the ends of the earth" (Acts 1:8). If you have committed your life to Jesus Christ, if he is your Lord and Savior, you have that power. You don't have to wait for it or work for it. That power is already yours through the Holy Spirit.

Even more amazing than the fact that we have such power available to us is the *nature* of the power we possess. Paul writes, "That power is the same as the mighty strength [God] exerted when he raised Christ from the dead and seated him at his right hand in the heavenly realms, far above all rule and authority, power and dominion, and every name that is invoked, not only in the present age but also in the one to come" (Ephesians 1:19-21).

The power that raised Jesus from the dead now lives in you. Not a sample or a portion of that power. Not a semblance of that power. The *same* resurrection power.

Paul says that when God raised Jesus from the dead, he also seated Jesus at his right hand in the heavenly realms. And here's a truly astounding thought: *We are seated in the heavenly realms with Jesus*—not only in the future, when we get to Heaven, but right now, at this very moment. Paul writes, "God raised us up with Christ and seated us with him in the heavenly realms in Christ Jesus" (Ephesians 2:6).

You might say, "I don't feel like I'm in the heavenly realms. I'm here in my ordinary, earthly place, doing my usual everyday things. What's so heavenly about where I am right now?"

Though it's true you may not *feel* heavenly at this moment, if you are in Christ, God looks at you and sees you already seated in the heavenly realms with Christ. He sees you as if you are already in Heaven.

Paul also gives us a glimpse into what it means that we are seated with Christ in the heavenly realms. He writes, "Do you not know that we will judge angels? How much more the things of this life!" (1 Corinthians 6:3). Isn't that amazing? God will entrust to us the right to judge the angels. So if we are already seated in the heavenly realm and destined to judge the angels, shouldn't we start living as true citizens of Heaven—and stop living as people who belong to this world?

So, how do we do this? How do we begin living as citizens of Heaven while we're still on earth? We begin by appropriating and exercising the power of God, moment by moment, day by day. We pray on a continual, ongoing basis, carrying on a conversation with God throughout the day, seeking his mind and his will, and asking him to accomplish his purpose through us. Whenever we have a conversation with another person, whenever we send an email or a text, whenever we post on social media, we can ask God to channel his power through us to touch the lives of others.

Throughout the day, think about your testimony before others. Think of your influence on others. How can you use the power God has given you to bless, comfort, and encourage other people? How can you use his power to reach the people around you for Jesus Christ? That power is already yours. Ask God to open your eyes for ways to use it.

You might say, "But I'm too shy to talk to other people about Jesus," or, "I don't have the spiritual gift of evangelism." Nonsense. Every Christian has a witness, every Christian has a personal story of what Jesus has done in his or her life. You don't have to *preach*. In fact, it's better if you don't. Just ask God to speak through you as you tell your story simply and honestly.

The problem so many Christians have with sharing the good news of Jesus with other people is that they tend to think it's up to them to convert other people. They think they're responsible to save souls. No, God calls us to be *witnesses*. What does a witness do in a court of law? A witness simply tells what they know to be true. It's the same principle when it comes to witnessing to others about Jesus.

It's not your job to convert people. You can't convert anyone anyway. That's the job of the Holy Spirit. It's the Spirit of God who convicts people of sin and their need of a Savior. But the Spirit uses people like you and me who are willing to share what they know. The Spirit uses people who are willing to love others where they are and bear witness to the power of God in their own lives.

When it comes to the dynamic power of God, all we have to do is light the fuse. It's the Holy Spirit's job to unleash that power in the direction he wants it to go.

Your Will Be Done

One of the most practical, transformative insights in the Bible is this line from the prayer Jesus taught his disciples to pray: "Your will be done, on earth as it is in heaven" (Matthew 6:10). The essence of the Christian life is knowing and doing God's will. If we would do the will of God moment by moment and day by day, we would be living our earthly lives as if we were already in Heaven.

Over the years, I've heard people express many bizarre and unbiblical notions about discerning the will of God. One particular incident stands out in my mind.

A man came to my office and said, "I know the Bible

teaches that God hates divorce. I've heard you preach on the subject, so I know what you think about divorce. But pastor, my situation is different. I know it's the will of God for me to divorce my wife and marry another woman."

This occurred many years ago, and I have to confess that I didn't respond with the level of wisdom that God gave me later in life. Trying hard to contain my shock and incredulity, I asked, "Well, tell me—how did you discover that this is the will of God for your life?"

"I thought it over," he said, "and I realized that God would not have allowed me to meet this other woman and fall in love with her if he didn't want us to be together. So, because God allowed me to meet her, I know he wants me to leave my present wife and marry the woman I fell in love with."

This man clearly understood what the Word of God teaches about divorce, about violating the marriage vow—yet he had convinced himself that God's clear commandments didn't apply to him. He planned to violate the Word of God and the will of God—and he was going to blame God for his actions. It was God's fault, he reasoned, for allowing him to meet this other woman.

One of the great regrets of my years of ministry is the way I responded to this man. Everything I said to him was biblically, morally true, but I said it without grace, without mercy. He never returned to our church and he never spoke to me again.

The reason I'm sharing this story with you is that I want you to understand and remember this principle: God will never tell you, through your circumstances, your conscience, or your emotions, to do anything that violates the clear teaching of his Word. God is unchanging. He is consistent. He will not say, "This commandment doesn't apply to you. You're exempt. It's my will for you to break this commandment."

If you think God is leading you to violate the clear teaching of his Word, then the voice you're hearing is not the voice of God. It is the temptation of Satan or the deception of your own selfish desires. Don't listen to that voice. If you want to do the will of God, then heed the Word of God.

Why is God's will good for us? Why is his will good for us even when we want to disobey it? For most people who profess to be Christians, doing the will of God does not sound very exciting. In fact, it sounds like drudgery. It sounds like a burden. It sounds like, "Do what you're told. Follow the rules. Submit and obey."

Yet, for those who truly love God, for those who faithfully walk with God day by day, there is no greater joy on earth than doing the will of God. There is no more liberating feeling than to obey and carry out God's will.

I have to confess that I have not always felt this way about the will of God. There was a time in my Christian life when I feared knowing the will of God for my life. Though I was a believer, my thinking was worldly and selfish. I was afraid that God would tell me to do something I didn't want to do.

Thank God, he helped me to gain the spiritual maturity to realize that it was Satan who put that fear in my heart. Don't let Satan give you a false view of God and his will.

There are many people in the church who truly think that God is out to get them. Over the years, I have talked with many people who view God that way. They think that God wants them to be miserable, that God is a killjoy. They fear God—and they fear his will. The prayerful words, "Your will be done, on earth as it is in heaven," stir a sense of dread and panic within them.

This is such a tragic condition for a believer to experience! The desire to obey God's will comes from an absolute conviction that he is good all the time. It comes from a settled assurance that God's will is rooted in his love for us.

Those who fear the will of God are the most likely to wander from God's plan for their lives—and there is no more dangerous place for a professing Christian than outside of God's will. As Jesus said, "Not everyone who says to me, 'Lord, Lord,' will enter the kingdom of heaven, but only the one who does the will of my Father who is in heaven" (Matthew 7:21). We can attend church and sing hymns and claim to love Jesus until we are blue in the face, but if we are not doing the will of God, as revealed in the Word of God, we are in spiritual jeopardy.

On Earth as It Is in Heaven

When Jesus taught his disciples to pray, "Your will be done, on earth as it is in heaven," he was imparting a life-changing principle. He wanted to transform the way we view our earthly lives. Most people recite those words without understanding what they are praying. But when we pray those words and truly mean them, we are asking God to produce a radical change in our lives.

This prayer runs counter to the mindset of our world today—including the mindset of the prevailing church culture today. Go to many churches and listen to the teaching there, and you'll hear a lot about how God is there to meet our needs. You'll hear a lot of teaching about all the things that God will do for us.

Politicians tell us that the government is there to meet our needs. Commercials tell us that if we just buy this or that product, our needs will be met. The church has largely fallen in line with the thinking of the surrounding culture. Contemporary North American churches largely cater to "felt needs," to the needs people consciously experience and express—the need for happiness, health, relationships, financial security, and so on.

But often the needs we feel are substitutes for our real needs, or our deepest need, which is a relationship with Jesus and citizenship in Heaven. Randy Alcorn, author of *Heaven*, says that we are all homesick for Heaven—and we often mistake that homesickness for some human want or need. He writes, "Nothing is more often misdiagnosed than our homesickness for Heaven. We think that what we want is sex, drugs, alcohol, a new job, a raise, a doctorate, a spouse, a large-screen television, a new car, a cabin in the woods, a condo in Hawaii. What we really want is the person we were made for, Jesus, and the place we were made for, Heaven. Nothing less can satisfy us."[2]

Felt needs are a bottomless pit. You can never satisfy your felt needs. But if you satisfy your real need, your need for Jesus, all your felt needs will fall into place.

Because our minds have been saturated with the "felt need" brainwashing of our culture, we often come to God in prayer with the wrong mindset. We pray, "God, what are you doing to meet my needs?"

But Jesus taught his disciples a very different pattern for prayer. The prayer begins, "Our Father in heaven." Jesus wants us to know that God is our Father, and he has a heavenly perspective on our lives. Then, "hallowed be your name." *Hallowed* means holy and sacred. Is the name of God honored and hallowed by the way you live your life? Then, "your kingdom come, your will be done, on earth as it is in heaven" (Matthew 6:9-10).

Notice that every one of those phrases at the beginning of the prayer is focused on God the Father, on the holiness of his name, on Heaven, and on the will of God. Nowhere in those phrases is there a plea for our needs to be met. The prayer opens with a total focus on God and his holy will.

Only after we have cleared our minds of earthly things and lifted our eyes to our Father in Heaven do we present our petitions to God: "Give us today our daily bread. And forgive us our debts, as we also have forgiven our debtors. And lead us not into temptation, but deliver us from the evil one" (Matthew 6:11-13).

Notice that Jesus doesn't encourage us to fill our prayers with a lot of felt needs. Nowhere does Jesus encourage us to pray, "Give me happiness. Give me a new relationship. Give me wealth." No, Jesus gives us a pattern of praying for our real needs. We need our daily bread. We need to be forgiven—and we need to forgive others. And we need to be delivered from temptation and from Satan. These are our deepest needs.

We often forget that God knows our needs before we do. And to prove it, God sent his Son to become a man and express real human needs. While on the earth, God the Son—who created the rivers, lakes, and oceans—said from the cross, "I am thirsty." He created the forests, yet he was nailed to a tree. He was the one who caused water to gush from a rock for Moses, yet he said to the Samaritan woman, "Give me a drink."

The Son of God became a man with real physical needs in order to show us that God knows our needs before we even ask him to meet them.

You might say, "If he knows our needs, then why should we ask him? Why do we need to pray?"

In the children's novel *The Magician's Nephew*, C. S. Lewis tells the story of the great lion Aslan (who represents Christ) sending two children, Polly and Digory, on a mission to obtain a healing apple from a tree in a distant valley. They speed through the air on a winged horse named Fledge. When they stop for the night, Polly and Digory realize they have nothing for dinner.

Digory indignantly says, "Well, I do think someone might have arranged about our meals."

Fledge the horse says, "I'm sure Aslan would have, if you'd asked him."

Polly says, "Wouldn't he know without being asked?"

Fledge wisely replies, "I've no doubt he would. But I've a sort of idea he likes to be asked."[3]

God cares about our real needs. He knows all about our needs even before we ask him. Even so, he likes to be asked.

And here's something interesting about the prayer Jesus taught us to pray: Jesus himself is the answer to that prayer. He taught us to pray, "Give us today our daily bread." Jesus is the Bread of Life. He taught us to pray, "Forgive us our debts." Jesus purchased our forgiveness on the cross. He taught us to pray, "As we also have forgiven our debtors." Jesus taught us to love and forgive our enemies, and he showed us how to forgive even as he was dying on the cross. He taught us to pray, "And lead us not into temptation, but deliver us from the evil one." Jesus gives us the victory over temptation, and he delivers us from Satan's power.

So let's pray after the pattern that Jesus taught us. Let's focus on God, our Father in Heaven, on his wonderful name, and on his will. Then let's ask him to meet our real needs, our deepest needs. If we pray the way Jesus taught us to pray, our "felt needs" will take care of themselves.

As Jesus also taught us, "Do not worry, saying, 'What shall we eat?' or 'What shall we drink?' or 'What shall we wear?' For the pagans run after all these things, and your heavenly Father knows that you need them. But seek first his kingdom and his righteousness, and all these things will be given to you as well" (Matthew 6:31-33).

How to Pray It and Mean It

At this point, there's a question I hope is uppermost in your mind: "How can I experience the joy and excitement of doing the will of God? How can I pray, 'Your kingdom come, your will be done, on earth as it is in heaven'—and really mean it?"

It all begins with our faith and trust in God. In order to pray "Your will be done" and mean it, we have to fully trust that God loves us and wants only the best for us. We have to believe that God is watching out for our good.

We also must acknowledge that God's view of what is best for us may not align with our own view. That's to be expected. God is our Father and we are his children. What do earthly children ask their earthly parents for? Sweets instead of vegetables. Screen time instead of homework time. Theme parks instead of chores. A lavish allowance and an expensive smartphone—but no rules, no responsibilities, no cares, no bedtime, and no discipline.

Just as children don't always see eye to eye with their parents about what is good for them, we don't always see eye to eye with God. And when he doesn't do what *we* think is in our best interest, when he delays in answering our prayers for this or that felt need, we question his love for us.

We cannot see over the horizon, but God can. We can only see today, but God sees all of eternity. What you think of as good might bring you misery in the future.

This may be hard for you to accept, but it's true: God sometimes protects us from our own prayers. As I look back over the countless prayers I have prayed, I thank God for the prayers he lovingly chose not to answer the way I wanted. I have prayed so many foolish prayers, so many selfish prayers. When God said *no* to those prayers, I sometimes assumed it was because he didn't love me. Now, in hindsight, I realize those unanswered prayers were God's deepest expression of his love. Had he indulged those foolish prayers, I might not be alive or serving him today.

When you fully trust the love of God, when you rest in the fact that he absolutely wants the best for you, then you can pray, "Your will be done," and really mean it.

But how do we build our faith and trust in God's love?

A good place to start is by bathing our minds in God's Word. We should begin each day by meditating on the love of God and the goodness of his will for our lives. We should write Scripture passages on cards and place them where we can see them throughout the day—on the bathroom mirror, next to the computer, on the refrigerator, on the dashboard of the car. Here are some beautiful Scripture passages to dwell on:

"How priceless is your unfailing love, O God! People take refuge in the shadow of your wings" (Psalm 36:7).

"Help me, Lord my God; save me according to your unfailing love" (Psalm 109:26).

"Let the morning bring me word of your unfailing love, for I have put my trust in you. Show me the way I should go, for to you I entrust my life" (Psalm 143:8).

"'Though the mountains be shaken and the hills be removed, yet my unfailing love for you will not be shaken nor my covenant of peace be removed,' says the LORD, who has compassion on you" (Isaiah 54:10).

"'For I know the plans I have for you,' declares the LORD, 'plans to prosper you and not to harm you, plans to give you hope and a future'" (Jeremiah 29:11).

"The LORD appeared to us in the past, saying: 'I have loved you with an everlasting love; I have drawn you with unfailing kindness'" (Jeremiah 31:3).

"Because of the LORD's great love we are not consumed, for his compassions never fail. They are new every morning; great is your faithfulness" (Lamentations 3:22-23).

"The LORD your God is with you, the Mighty Warrior who saves. He will take great delight in you; in his love he will no longer rebuke you, but will rejoice over you with singing" (Zephaniah 3:17).

"I am convinced that neither death nor life, neither angels nor demons, neither the present nor the future, nor any powers, neither height nor depth, nor anything else in all creation, will be able to separate us from the love of God that is in Christ Jesus our Lord" (Romans 8:38-39).

"Cast all your anxiety on him because he cares for you" (1 Peter 5:7).

"This is how God showed his love among us: He sent his one and only Son into the world that we might live through him. This is love: not that we loved God, but that he loved us and sent his Son as an atoning sacrifice for our sins" (1 John 4:9-10).

"And so we know and rely on the love God has for us. God is love. Whoever lives in love lives in God, and God in them" (1 John 4:16).

Living in Heaven Right Now

I love to talk about Heaven. Next to Jesus himself, Heaven is my favorite subject. I could talk about Jesus and Heaven all day long and deep into the night. I rejoice whenever I get to tell others about Heaven. I make all of my plans and conduct all of my activities with Heaven in mind.

Having God's perspective on Heaven is essential to living a triumphant Christian life here on earth. We desperately need to live each day in light of Paul's words in 2 Corinthians 4:18: "We fix our eyes not on what is seen, but on what is unseen, since what is seen is temporary, but what is unseen is eternal." If this described our moment-by-moment perspective, it would radically transform our thoughts, our speech, and our behavior.

An awareness of our citizenship in Heaven motivates us to witness about Jesus boldly and without inhibition. It motivates us to persevere through trials and opposition, cheerfully and without resentment. It motivates us to serve God with glad and grateful hearts. It motivates us to bless and forgive our enemies. It motivates us to watch the news without bitterness or rage or fear, because we know that this world and its evils are passing away. It motivates us to serve God and others, eagerly and generously, in order to speed the day of the Lord's return.

As Joni Eareckson Tada writes in *Heaven: Your Real Home*, "When Christians realize that their citizenship is in heaven, they begin acting as responsible citizens of earth. They invest wisely in relationships because they know they're eternal. Their conversations, goals, and motives become pure and honest because they realize these will have a bearing on everlasting reward. They give generously of time, money, and talent because they are laying up treasures for eternity. They spread the good news of Christ because they long to fill heaven's ranks with their friends and neighbors. All this serves the pilgrims well, not only in heaven, but on earth, for it serves everyone around them."[4]

The most important way the knowledge of Heaven affects our present lives is that it requires us to make a decision: Do we *accept* Christ and Heaven—or do we *reject* Christ and Heaven? There is no middle ground. We must decide. Failure to decide is, in fact, a decision to be eternally separated from God.

Jesus said, "Enter through the narrow gate. For wide is the gate and broad is the road that leads to destruction, and many enter through it. But small is the gate and narrow the road that leads to life, and only a few find it" (Matthew 7:13-14).

Heaven is reserved for those who have made a decision for Christ alone. Heaven is reserved only for those who love Jesus and serve Jesus and obey Jesus in this life. Heaven is reserved for all who acknowledge their sin and who have accepted the free gift of salvation that is found only in the blood of Jesus shed for our sins.

If you have not yet made that decision, I urge you to do it today, right now, before it's too late. You don't have to wait until you die to discover the joys of Heaven. You can begin to experience Heaven right here on earth. The Bible tells us that God is "is patient with you, not wanting anyone to perish, but everyone to come to repentance" (2 Peter 3:9). God's will for your life is that you would live forever with him in Heaven.

May God's will be done in your life, on earth as it is in Heaven.

WARNING & the PROMISE the

part 3

9

WARNING! WARNING! WARNING!

THERE IS A STORY TOLD ABOUT C. S. Lewis that may or may not be true. I haven't been able to find a published source for the anecdote. However, it certainly sounds like something Lewis would have said and done.

According to the story, Lewis went to church to hear a newly ordained Anglican curate preach. In the Church of England, a curate is someone who has just come out of seminary and is new in the ministry. This young curate preached a sermon urging people to accept Jesus as their Lord and Savior.

"If you reject Jesus Christ as Savior and Lord," the young preacher said, "you will suffer grave eschatological ramifications."

After the service, Lewis went to the young man and said, "Did you mean to say that those who reject Jesus Christ will spend eternity in Hell?"

"Yes, that's exactly right, sir."

"Then why didn't you just say so?"

When it comes to serious matters like eternity in Hell, we dare not cloud the issue with phrases like "grave eschatological ramifications." Nothing beats straight talk.

Hell is not a popular subject in today's pulpits. Many preachers never preach about Hell at any time in their ministry. I believe preachers who avoid the subject of Hell are doing their congregations a terrible disservice.

Though Hell is not a popular subject among Christian preachers and writers today, it's important to understand that God grants us freedom of choice. We have the choice to believe in him and be reconciled to God the Father through his Son, Jesus Christ—or we can reject him and end up in eternal torment.

In Acts 17:30-31, Paul says that God "commands all people everywhere to repent" because he "has set a day when he will judge the world with justice." The reality of God's judgment and the certainty of Hell should fill us with a sense of urgency to spread the gospel and warn the people around us to seek refuge in Jesus Christ.

In 2 Thessalonians 2:3, Paul tells us that, immediately before the return of Christ, there will be a tidal wave of rebellion and sin across the globe. And Jesus, while explaining future events to his disciples on the Mount of Olives, said

that, before his return, there will be intense hatred and persecution against Christians: "Then you will be handed over to
be persecuted and put to death, and you will be hated by all
nations because of me. . . . Because of the increase of wicked-
ness, the love of most will grow cold" (Matthew 24:9, 12).

Satan's Time Grows Short

Today, it is becoming increasingly dangerous to follow Jesus.
According to *Christianity Today*, on any given day, thirteen Christians are killed for their faith, a dozen churches
or Christian buildings are attacked, a dozen Christians are
unjustly jailed for their faith, and five Christians are abducted
somewhere in the world.[1] We know that persecution of the
church is most extreme in countries such as North Korea,
Afghanistan, Pakistan, and China. But we are also seeing a
rising spirit of anti-Christian persecution and anarchy perme-
ating every culture, every society, in every part of the world.

Hatred toward God and his children is on the rise. The
demonic rage against God's church is just the beginning.
Why? Because Satan and his demons know that their time
is growing short. They know that, as the book of Revelation
promises, Satan and his followers will be "thrown into the
lake of burning sulfur" and they "will be tormented day and
night for ever and ever" (Revelation 20:10).

Think about what "for ever and ever" means. The
great deceiver who lured children into rebellion and self-
destruction will be tormented day and night for ever and
ever. The great deceiver who lured husbands and wives into

destroying their marriages and families will be tormented day and night for ever and ever. The great deceiver who fooled people into thinking that God does not love them, that they can be good people without God, will be tormented day and night for ever and ever. The great deceiver who tempts people into stealing and murdering and destroying lives and reputations will, along with all his cronies, be tormented day and night for ever and ever in the lake of fire.

God did not create Hell as a place of punishment for human beings. He created Hell for Satan and his demons. The demons don't have a choice. They cannot be saved and forgiven by God's grace. They are already condemned.

But you and I can choose our eternal destination. God urges every man, every woman, every child to repent, to receive forgiveness, to accept the free gift of salvation—because he has appointed a day on which he will judge the world.

A Hint of What Was to Come

Throughout his earthly ministry, Jesus was preparing his disciples for the time when he would be crucified, resurrected, and ascended. He was preparing them to minister in his name after he had left the earth. In the final hours before his crucifixion, he was still preparing them, teaching them, and encouraging them.

In the Gospel of John, there is a scene that often goes unnoticed. It takes place in those final hours before Jesus goes to the cross: "There were some Greeks among those who went up to worship at the festival. They came to Philip, who was from Bethsaida in Galilee, with a request. 'Sir,' they said, 'we would like to see Jesus.' Philip went to tell Andrew; Andrew and Philip in turn told Jesus" (John 12:20-22).

Who were these Greeks who wanted to see Jesus? They were Gentiles who worshiped God. They had heard about Yahweh, the God of Israel, and they wanted to know him and worship him; but because they were not ethnically Jewish, they were not full partakers of God's covenant with Israel. So these Greeks came to Jerusalem for the Passover celebration, and they heard about Jesus and his teachings and his mighty works. They went to his disciples and said, "Please, we want to see Jesus."

How does Jesus respond to this news from Philip and Andrew? Does he tell them, "Show these Greek fellows in?" No, Jesus makes a statement that seems strangely at odds with the request that Philip and Andrew have brought to him: "The hour has come for the Son of Man to be glorified. Very truly I tell you, unless a kernel of wheat falls to the ground and dies, it remains only a single seed. But if it dies, it produces many seeds" (John 12:23-24).

I don't think Jesus was ignoring the request from the Greeks. He was responding to their request. He was saying, in effect, "The hour has come for my death, for my glorification. Even the Greeks—the non-Jewish Gentiles—have come to seek me out. When I have been crucified, resurrected, and glorified, salvation will be offered not only to the Jewish nation, but to people from every nation on earth."

Jesus goes on to say, "Now is the time for judgment on this world; now the prince of this world will be driven out. And I, when I am lifted up from the earth, will draw all people to myself" (John 12:31-32). Who is the prince of this world? It is Satan, of course. And when Jesus is raised up on the cross, Satan will be defeated, cast out—and then Jesus will draw all people, from around the world, to himself.

Later, in the book of Acts, after the resurrected Jesus ascends into Heaven, we see Peter preach in Jerusalem on the Day of Pentecost. On that day, the newly founded church welcomes hundreds of believers—not just Jews and Greeks, but also "Parthians, Medes and Elamites; residents of Mesopotamia, Judea and Cappadocia, Pontus and Asia, Phrygia and Pamphylia, Egypt and the parts of Libya near Cyrene; visitors from Rome (both Jews and converts to Judaism); Cretans and Arabs" (Acts 2:9-11).

The Greeks who wanted to meet Jesus in the final hours before his crucifixion provided a hint of what was to come. The good news of Jesus Christ would soon travel across the globe.

Today, we see the church of Jesus Christ in every corner of the world. The church spans the earth and ministers to every culture and ethnic group around the planet. People are coming to Christ under the most severe and difficult circumstances. God is preparing his church for the return of Jesus.

Ever since the Crucifixion, Satan stands condemned and sentenced to eternal damnation in the lake of fire. It's just a matter of time until that sentence is carried out.

At his first coming, Jesus bound the demonic powers. At his second coming, he will release all of his children from satanic oppression.

At his first coming, Jesus raised a few people from the dead—the son of a widow in the village of Nain, the young daughter of Jairus in Capernaum, and his friend Lazarus in Bethany. They all died again. At his second coming, Jesus will raise all his children into life everlasting.

Satan's Least Favorite Subject

Some people complain about—or make fun of—so-called fire-and-brimstone preachers who are always talking about Hell. But do you know who the first fire-and-brimstone preacher was? Jesus himself. So we need to make sure that, if we complain about such preachers and their teachings about Hell, we are not criticizing the preaching of Jesus.

I once preached a sermon called "The Anatomy of Hell," one of many sermons I have preached on that subject. After the service, a man came to me with a troubled expression. He said, "Michael, Hell is such a negative and frightening thing. Why do you even talk about that subject?"

"Because," I said, "it's Satan's least favorite topic. He hates hearing about it. Satan doesn't want to be reminded of his future. Satan does not want preachers to warn people about Hell, because he wants a lot of people to spend eternity with him in the lake of fire. I warn people about Hell because Jesus warned people about hell—and that makes Satan furious."

Satan loves it when people joke about Hell and trivialize

Hell and fail to take it seriously. You will never see me joke about Hell in my writing or my preaching. When I write or preach about Hell, I do so with grief in my heart. I visualize people to whom I have witnessed, people who have rejected the gospel, and I'm saddened that they are going to end up in Hell for all eternity.

With the 1970 release of the hit single "I'm Eighteen," singer Alice Cooper (the stage name adopted by Vincent Furnier) became famous for his gravelly voice, his pyrotechnic shows, and his use of snakes as stage props. His wild shows earned him the title of "Godfather of Shock Rock." But there was a time when Cooper's use of drugs and alcohol began to scare him—and he realized he was on his way to ending up dead like so many other rock stars.

In a 2019 YouTube interview with pastor Greg Laurie, Cooper recalled that he looked in the mirror and saw blood coming from his eyes—though it might have been a hallucination. He flushed the drugs down the toilet and went to bed for three days to kick his habit. Then he called his wife, who had left him, and told her he was through with drugs. She agreed to return to him if he would go to church with her.

Cooper began going to church with his wife in Phoenix. The pastor, he recalled, "was a Hell's fire pastor" and those sermons about Hell scared Cooper into giving his life to Jesus Christ. "You know," he said, "a lot of people say, 'I came to Christ because my love of Jesus.' I came to Christ because of my fear of God. I totally understood that Hell . . . was going to be the worst place ever. In fear I came back to the Lord."[2]

It is no pleasure, I assure you, to talk about Hell. But I must preach and teach the whole truth of God and his Word. And that means I must talk about Hell.

The Source of Our Knowledge about Hell

Almost everything we know about Hell comes from Jesus. In fact, Jesus spoke more about Heaven and Hell than anybody in the Bible. He spoke more about Hell than he spoke about Heaven. That ought to tell us something about the importance of understanding Hell.

Jesus spoke about Hell in the some of the most urgent, vivid, and descriptive language you will find in Scripture. Though he spoke frequently and compellingly about Hell, it was not to frighten or coerce people. Instead, he wanted to warn people—in the most caring, heartbroken, and compassionate way—so they would turn to him and be saved.

Why was Jesus so concerned about Hell? Because he knows what it will be like there. As the Creator of the universe, he knows that Hell was prepared as the destination for Satan and his demons. That's why he continually pleaded with people to repent and accept God's plan for salvation. He implored people to take refuge in him and in his cross, because the wrath of God was about to be revealed.

Read the words of Jesus when he talks about judgment. You'll never hear him speak with hostility or in anger. Both Matthew 23:37-39 and Luke 19:41-44 record the scene where Jesus weeps over Jerusalem. He weeps because he foresees the judgment that would come upon Jerusalem in AD

70, when the Roman general Titus would lay siege to the city, bringing about the total destruction of the city and the Temple, and the death of thousands of people. Jesus wept over the fact that the people had rejected him and sealed their doom. They rejected the only way to Heaven and eternal life.

What Jesus Taught about Hell

I once had a conversation with a neighbor, a man who attended church and considered himself a good Christian. He told me, "I believe that all religions lead to the same place. Jesus taught us to love everybody, and I can't believe a loving God would send anyone to Hell." I quoted Scripture to the man, I reasoned with him from God's Word, and I was literally in tears as I tried to explain the truth to him—but he was convinced that all religions lead to God, and he wouldn't listen to God's own Word on the subject.

Many people have an impression of God as an indulgent, grandfatherly figure who looks the other way when we sin. Such people view Jesus as a meek, mild, milquetoast kind of person—a benign and harmless man whose message was essentially, "Love everybody."

We must always remember that Jesus is the second person of the Trinity. He is God in human flesh. He is God the Son, who coexisted with God the Father before all the worlds were created. He left the splendor of Heaven and came to earth to redeem every repentant, confessing sinner.

He is the Lord of mercy and grace, but we should always remember that he is also the Lord of justice, the one who will judge all of humanity. And we must acknowledge that the judgment of unrepentant sinners leads to Hell.

The Bible makes it very clear that Hell is a real place. Hell is not a state of mind, not a figment of the imagination, not a figure of speech. Hell is a real place and real people are going to be there for all eternity. Jesus was explicit in describing the intense suffering of those who end up there.

Was it God's plan to create Hell as a place of punishment for human beings? No. Jesus states clearly that Hell is "the eternal fire prepared for the devil and his angels" (Matthew 25:41).

Jesus also makes it clear that Hell is a place of confinement. In Matthew 18:21-35, he describes Hell as a prison— not a physical prison, but a prison of the soul and spirit. A physical prison can only imprison the body, but it cannot imprison the mind, soul, or spirit. When Paul was in prison, his body was confined, yet he was free to worship, sing, pray, hope, and write powerful letters under the inspiration of the Holy Spirit. But a soul imprisoned in Hell is truly confined in every way imaginable.

If you have visited Venice, Italy, you may have taken a canal boat ride down the Rio di Palazzo, passing under an enclosed bridge carved from white limestone called the Bridge of Sighs. That bridge, built from 1600 to 1603 with stone-barred windows, connects the interrogation rooms of the Doge's palace to the prison known as Prigioni Nuove. When prisoners passed from the interrogation rooms across the Bridge of Sighs, they would look out through the stone-barred windows and catch their last glimpse of Venice before spending the rest of their lives in prison—and that is why the prisoners would sigh. When prisoners crossed the Bridge of Sighs, they knew they would never cross back. They were going to a place of permanent confinement.

Jesus tells us that Hell will be a place of everlasting confinement. There is no release, no appeal, no going back.

Next, Jesus tells us that Hell is a place of utter darkness. In both Matthew 22:13 and Matthew 25:30, Jesus describes Hell as "the darkness, where there will be weeping and gnashing of teeth." Hell is outer darkness, perpetual darkness. In Hell there will be no day—just eternal darkness. And it will not only be a physical, experiential darkness, but it will be a moral and spiritual darkness as well—a complete absence of the presence and goodness of God. Those consigned to Hell will experience constant agony and relentless regret.

Imprisoned Spirits

In Luke 16:19-31, we find the account of a rich man and a beggar named Lazarus. Some people believe this story is a parable that Jesus told to teach a spiritual lesson. But this is not a parable. It's a true account. Jesus never calls this story a parable. Instead, he says, "There was a rich man who was dressed in purple and fine linen and lived in luxury every day. At his gate was laid a beggar named Lazarus" (Luke 16:19-20).

This is the only story Jesus told in which he names an individual in the story: Lazarus. In all his other parables,

WARNING! WARNING! WARNING!

Jesus uses a commonplace earthly experience or object—a farmer, a wedding, a lost coin, a lost sheep, a fig tree—to teach a spiritual lesson. But the setting for this account is neither commonplace nor earthly; it is the afterlife.

When Jesus talked about Lazarus and the rich man, he told a true story of actual events—events that he would know about—as the God of the universe who existed eternally before his incarnation. He presents the rich man as selfish, with no compassion for the poor. Lazarus was a poor man who died outside the rich man's gate.

When Lazarus and the rich man both died, in death they experienced a reversal of fortunes. The rich man, who had enjoyed selfish pleasures all his life, ended up in a place of agony. Lazarus, after a lifetime of suffering and poverty, ended up at the side of Abraham.

This is how people viewed the afterlife in Old Testament times. Luke 16:23 tells us that the rich man was in Hades. This is the actual Greek word—*hades*—that appears in the original text. The Hebrew word for Hades is *Sheol*, the place where the spirits of the dead went to await the final judgment.

The apostle Peter tells us, "After being made alive, he [Jesus] went and made proclamation to the imprisoned spirits—to those who were disobedient long ago" (1 Peter 3:19-20). In other words, the resurrected Lord Jesus went to Hades (*Sheol*), the place of the spirits of the dead, and he liberated all the Old Testament believers there. He took them into Paradise and opened Heaven for them.

As Jesus pictures Hades in the account of Lazarus and the

rich man, there is one section for believers such as Abraham, who lived faithfully, looking forward to the arrival of Jesus the Messiah. The other section of Hades was reserved for those who refused to believe and practice the faith of Abraham. There was a huge gulf or chasm between these two sections of Hades. Yet the rich man was able to see and communicate with Abraham and Lazarus across this chasm.

The rich man was in constant pain. He said, "Father Abraham, have pity on me and send Lazarus to dip the tip of his finger in water and cool my tongue, because I am in agony in this fire" (Luke 16:24). He used the title "Father Abraham" because he held the common and mistaken view that Abraham was on his side because he was ethnically Jewish. But the truth is that only those who are *spiritual* descendants of Abraham, those who live by faith in Jesus, will be accepted into Heaven. Ethnicity means nothing; faith in Jesus means everything.

When you read these words of the rich man—"I am in agony in this fire"—you can see why I don't enjoy the subject of Hell. You can also see why I feel compelled to speak out and write about Hell, because I don't want anyone to have to spend a moment in Hell, much less an eternity.

Note the irony of this moment in the story: The rich man never lifted a finger to minister to the sufferings of Lazarus or anyone else, but now he begs Abraham to send Lazarus to dip his finger in water to cool his tongue and ease his suffering. But Abraham replies that Lazarus can't go to the rich man because "a great chasm has been set in place," preventing anyone from crossing over.

Next, the rich man says to Abraham, "Then I beg you, father, send Lazarus to my family, for I have five brothers. Let him warn them, so that they will not also come to this place of torment" (Luke 16:27-28). After only minutes in Hell, the rich man had become an evangelist. He wanted Lazarus to rise from the dead and warn his brothers. But Abraham told the rich man that Lazarus could not go to his brothers.

In this account, Jesus describes the nature of Hell in great detail. It's a place of confinement, a place of darkness and suffering, and a place of loneliness and regret.

The Inhabitants of Hell

In popular culture, we sometimes hear people say they look forward to being in Hell with all their friends, where they can carouse and drink and get high. They have bought one of Satan's cleverest lies—that the very debauchery and sin that condemned them to Hell can still be enjoyed there in the company of their friends. But Hell will be a place of absolute loneliness and isolation.

Philosopher Friedrich Nietzsche is reported to have said, "In Heaven all the interesting people are missing."[3] In other words, all the people Nietzsche thought were interesting to know and talk to and spend time with were in Hell, not Heaven.

But look at the list—and it's only a very partial list—of

people the Bible says will be in Hell: "The cowardly, the unbelieving, the vile, the murderers, the sexually immoral, those who practice magic arts, the idolaters and all liars—they will be consigned to the fiery lake of burning sulfur. This is the second death" (Revelation 21:8). Do these sound like "interesting people" you would like to spend eternity with—or even spend an evening with?

Remember, though, that the inhabitants of Hell will not be enjoying fellowship with each other. They will not be seeing each other and talking to each other. Hell is a place of solitary confinement. Everyone is alone. Everyone is isolated. All feelings of attachment, friendship, and love are forgotten forever.

When the eternal stakes are this high, why would anyone risk his or her eternal future? And why would you allow any friend or loved one to go into eternity without talking to them about Heaven and Hell?

To be quite candid, it exhausts my spirit to write at this length about Hell. It saddens me and fills me with a deep melancholy to write about these matters. But I write these words out of obedience to my Lord—and out of love for lost people.

I don't want to end this book on the subject of the destination of unbelievers. Instead, I want to close by focusing once again on the destination of all believers. I love that subject so much more than the subject we've been talking about.

If you have committed your life to Jesus Christ as your Savior and Lord, you do not have to worry about Hell. You are going to Heaven. You may be weary of fighting the good fight of faith. You may be exhausted from standing your spiritual ground and refusing to compromise with Satan and the world and the godless culture. But don't give up. You are going to a very real, physical place called Heaven.

You may have noticed that the same people who lie about Hell also lie about Heaven. They say that Heaven is just a state of mind. Or Heaven is a theological abstraction. Or Heaven is a metaphor, a figure of speech. Or Heaven is just wishful thinking.

Don't you believe it! The Word of God is unambiguously clear on this: Heaven is a real, physical place, and the destination of all believers.

In John 14:1-2, Jesus says, "Do not let your hearts be troubled. You believe in God; believe also in me. My Father's house has many rooms; if that were not so, would I have told you that I am going there to prepare a place for you?" The Greek word Jesus uses for "place" is *topos*. In the Greek language, *topos* means "a physical location." It means a real place with boundaries, dimensions, volume, and space.

Jesus is not preparing a state of mind for us. He is not preparing a metaphor for us. He is preparing a *place* for us.

In Acts 7, Stephen, the first Christian martyr, is on trial before the members of the Sanhedrin. After he testifies to them about Jesus—the very one they had unjustly condemned to death by crucifixion—the men of the Sanhedrin become enraged. At that moment, the Holy Spirit grants Stephen a powerful vision of his approaching destination.

"Look," Stephen said. "I see heaven open and the Son of Man standing at the right hand of God" (Acts 7:56).

Hearing this, the men of the Sanhedrin rushed Stephen, dragged him out of the city, and stoned him to death. Yet the Spirit had given Stephen a glimpse of his eternal destiny. What Stephen saw in the closing moments of his life is the scene all followers of Jesus Christ will see as soon as they close their eyes in death.

It's the same scene the apostle John describes in the book of Revelation: "I looked, and there before me was a door standing open in heaven" (Revelation 4:1). This vision of Heaven is what we must fix our eyes on and rest our hopes upon.

Hell is a tragic reality, and we must warn everyone around us, and show them how to escape it. Thank God, our great and unshakable reality as believers is eternity in Heaven with Jesus.

10

WHEN WILL JESUS RETURN?

Two days before Jesus was crucified, he stood on the Mount of Olives with his disciples and taught them about the last days. He taught them about a far-future day when he would return to judge the world.

Some of what he taught that day he stated openly and plainly. But most of his teaching about his second coming was in the form of parables. He told them "the parable of the ten virgins," the theme of which is to be prepared and watchful for Jesus' unexpected return (Matthew 25:1-13).

Jesus began the parable by saying that the Kingdom of Heaven will be like ten bridesmaids who are waiting for the bridegroom to arrive to start the wedding banquet. Five of the bridesmaids are wise and five are foolish.

One of the responsibilities of a bridesmaid in those days was to hold a ceremonial lamp to shed a beautiful glow on the wedding banquet. The wise bridesmaids had jars of extra oil for their lamps, but the foolish bridesmaids had forgotten to bring oil for their lamps.

While they were waiting for the bridegroom to arrive, all ten bridesmaids fell asleep. Then, at midnight, someone shouted, "Here's the bridegroom! Come out to meet him!"

With the arrival of the bridegroom, the wedding was about to begin. All ten bridesmaids arose and trimmed their lamps—but the five foolish bridesmaids had no oil left. They were unable to light their lamps—and the wise bridesmaids knew better than to share their oil with the foolish bridesmaids. They had just enough oil and no more.

In a panic, the five foolish bridesmaids rushed out to buy more oil, and while they were gone, the wedding banquet began. The door was shut. The five foolish bridesmaids were locked out. When they returned, they shouted, "Lord, Lord, open the door for us!"

But the lord of the banquet replied, "Truly I tell you, I don't know you."

Jesus concluded his story with these words: "Therefore keep watch, because you do not know the day or the hour."

This parable is not difficult to interpret. The ten bridesmaids, of course, represent all who profess to be believers, including you and me. The question is: Are we among the wise bridesmaids or the foolish ones?

All Christians are supposed to be awaiting the return of Jesus. But are we preparing for his return? Are we looking forward to Jesus coming back to take us to Heaven? Have we filled our jars with oil so that we will be ready for the wedding banquet in Heaven? Have we been faithful and active in obeying the Lord and working for the Kingdom?

The oil in the parable represents all the good works, all the faithfulness, all the prayerfulness, all the obedience that we have stored up during our earthly lives. Christians have been looking for the return of Jesus for centuries, and many believers wonder why he is taking so long to return. The Bridegroom appears to be late, but that doesn't mean he isn't coming.

Jesus will return right on schedule, according to the timetable of God the Father. We need to be ready, or else we risk being locked out of the wedding banquet in Heaven.

Understand that when Jesus speaks of the door being shut, he is talking about the door of Heaven. Anyone left outside the door will be in Hell, separated from God forever. That is why the lord of the banquet says, "I don't know you." There is no return from Hell. There is no second chance. The door is shut and God says, "I don't know you."

I urge you, I plead with you, please do not be like the foolish bridesmaids in the parable. Wake up! Prepare yourself for Jesus' return!

The Bridegroom may arrive at any moment. Are you ready?

The Sheep and the Goats

During that same discussion on the Mount of Olives, Jesus told another parable about the last days. It is a parable of a time when God will separate the believers from the unbelievers, the saved from the lost, the "sheep" from the "goats."

Jesus tells the disciples, "When the Son of Man comes in his glory, and all the angels with him, he will sit on his glorious throne. All the nations will be gathered before him, and he will separate the people one from another as a shepherd separates the sheep from the goats. He will put the sheep on his right and the goats on his left" (Matthew 25:31-33).

Here, Jesus describes his role as the King of the Kingdom of Heaven. He will say to those on his right, the sheep, "Come, you who are blessed by my Father; take your inheritance, the kingdom prepared for you since the creation of the world. For I was hungry and you gave me something to eat, I was thirsty and you gave me something to drink, I was a stranger and you invited me in, I needed clothes and you clothed me, I was sick and you looked after me, I was in prison and you came to visit me" (Matthew 25:34-36).

And the righteous believers, the sheep, will say, "Lord, when did we see you hungry and feed you, or thirsty and give you something to drink? When did we see you a stranger and invite you in, or needing clothes and clothe you? When did we see you sick or in prison and go to visit you?" (Matthew 25:37-39).

And King Jesus will reply, "Truly I tell you, whatever you

did for one of the least of these brothers and sisters of mine, you did for me" (Matthew 25:40).

Here again, Jesus focuses our attention on the works we do in this life that prepare us for the life to come. If we are spreading the good news of the Kingdom and meeting the needs of the hungry and thirsty and poor and sick and imprisoned, then we are his sheep. We are preparing ourselves in this life for an eternity in Heaven.

But, Jesus says, he will then turn to those on his left, the goats, and say, "Depart from me, you who are cursed, into the eternal fire prepared for the devil and his angels. For I was hungry and you gave me nothing to eat, I was thirsty and you gave me nothing to drink, I was a stranger and you did not invite me in, I needed clothes and you did not clothe me, I was sick and in prison and you did not look after me" (Matthew 25:41-43).

Then, Jesus concludes, "Then they will go away to eternal punishment, but the righteous to eternal life" (Matthew 25:46).

Sheep are gentle creatures who love to follow the shepherd. Goats, on the other hand, are stubborn and unruly animals. They love to go their own way and butt heads with each other. Goats often aggravate the sheep and lead them astray.

A herd of sheep and a herd of goats may look alike to a city slicker, but not to a shepherd. In the Middle East, goats and sheep often graze together in the same fields. Goats sometimes mix in with the sheep herds. From a distance, you can't tell the goats from the sheep. But Jesus knows his sheep.

On the Judgment Day, he will separate them from the goats and lead them into eternal life.

Jesus often spoke of his sheep, but he never said, "My goats listen to my voice." He said, "My sheep listen to my voice; I know them, and they follow me" (John 10:27).

This is an important distinction between sheep and goats: The sheep know the voice of their shepherd; but to a goat, one shepherd is as good as another. Goats have no discernment or loyalty. For a goat, all paths lead to the same destination.

The Great Separation

The goats in this parable represent people who think they are religious, think they are saved, and think they are righteous, but who are not. They have lived their lives without serving Jesus, without meeting the needs of the people around them. They have neglected to feed the hungry, shelter strangers, and minister to the sick and imprisoned—and they missed their chance to minister to Jesus himself.

Is Jesus saying that good works get you into Heaven? No. Throughout his ministry, Jesus made it clear that salvation is a free gift, paid for by his blood, which we simply accept by faith. Good works do not qualify us for salvation. Good works are the *result* of salvation. If we are truly saved, if we are truly his sheep, then we will *want* to feed the hungry, offer shelter to strangers, and minister to the poor. We will *want* to live as imitators of Jesus.

Jesus will instantly know his sheep, those who are his

genuine followers. His sheep are indwelled by the Holy Spirit. Because the Spirit lives in them, the sheep naturally want to serve God, love others, and give of themselves. They don't even think they are doing anything unusual or special. Good deeds are simply the natural result of being the sheep of the Lord's pasture.

When Jesus comes to separate the sheep from the goats, the process will be simple and straightforward: sheep on the right, goats on the left. Those who have genuinely followed the Good Shepherd with sheeplike devotion will be on the right; those who were stubborn, goat-headed, and selfish will be on the left.

If you have committed your life to the Lord Jesus, if you have repented of your sin and have been forgiven by God, you have nothing to fear from the great separation of the sheep and the goats. You are a sheep.

But if you have decided to remake God in your own image, if you think God owes you eternal life because of your good works, if you feel entitled to go to Heaven because your so-called good deeds outweigh your bad deeds, then I'm sorry to have to tell you this, but you, my friend, are a goat. You have rejected God's plan of salvation. You have rejected God's Son, the Lord Jesus, and you have refused God's plan of salvation.

"I don't need God, I can save myself." That's how goats think.

I urge you, while there is still time, to go to Jesus in repentance and humility. The Day of Judgment is coming quickly, but there is still time. Jesus could return in the next few moments or in a thousand years—but you need to be ready right now, today. You may be a goat as you read these words—but there is still time to become a sheep.

As Paul writes, "[God] says, 'In the time of my favor I heard you, and in the day of salvation I helped you.' I tell you, now is the time of God's favor, now is the day of salvation" (2 Corinthians 6:2).

The parable of the sheep and the goats demands that we examine ourselves. Take time to look deeply within and ask, "When Jesus returns, will I be on his right hand or his left? Will I be among the sheep, or among the goats?"

The Book of Life

When Jesus returns, he will judge the human race. As he himself said, "Just as the Father raises the dead and gives them life, even so the Son gives life to whom he is pleased to give it. Moreover, the Father judges no one, but has entrusted all judgment to the Son, that all may honor the Son just as they honor the Father" (John 5:21-23).

During his days on earth, Jesus lived and died in humility. But a day is coming when he will rule the nations with a rod of iron. The Crucified One will take his throne as the King of Heaven and the Judge of the earth. Only those who worship and serve King Jesus will become citizens of Heaven, subjects of the Kingdom of God.

Many people prefer to think of Jesus as meek and mild. They don't like the image of a Jesus who would come to judge the human race. But people who think this way are looking through the wrong end of the telescope. They shouldn't be surprised that Jesus will judge sinners. Instead, they should be amazed that he humbled himself to die on a cross to purchase our pardon and forgiveness.

The judgment of humanity will begin when Jesus comes in power and glory. As John writes, "I saw a great white throne and him who was seated on it. The earth and the heavens fled from his presence, and there was no place for them. And I saw the dead, great and small, standing before the throne, and books were opened. Another book was opened, which is the book of life. The dead were judged according to what they had done as recorded in the books" (Revelation 20:11-12).

The first mention of the Book of Life is in Psalm 69. There, David cries out to God that he is drowning in a sea of trouble. His enemies are arrayed against him, and he begs God to take up his cause and defend him against his foes. He writes of his enemies, "Charge them with crime upon crime; do not let them share in your salvation. May they be blotted out of the book of life and not be listed with the righteous" (Psalm 69:27-28).

Paul, in his letter to the Philippians, commends "Clement and the rest of my co-workers, whose names are in the book of life" (Philippians 4:3).

Revelation refers to the Book of Life six times, including twice in Revelation 20: "I saw the dead, great and small, standing before the throne, and books were opened. Another book was opened, which is the book of life. The dead were judged according to what they had done as recorded in the books. . . . Anyone whose name was not found written in the book of life was thrown into the lake of fire" (Revelation 20:12, 15).

Jesus described the scene that will take place on the Day of Judgment: "Many will say to me on that day, 'Lord, Lord, did we not prophesy in your name and in your name drive out demons and in your name perform many miracles?' Then I will tell them plainly, 'I never knew you. Away from me, you evildoers!'" (Matthew 7:22-23). That is such a sobering scene. Those people will address Jesus as Lord, and yet he will say he never knew them. I can picture it in my imagination.

"Lord, Lord, I went to church many times!"

"Your name is not written in the Book of Life."

"Lord, Lord, I did many good works!"

"Your name is not written in the Book of Life."

"Lord, Lord, I was a good person, a nice person, not a bad person!"

"Your name is not written in the Book of Life."

What a tragic day that will be for countless souls, for countless people who never gave much thought to eternity, for countless people who assumed they were good people and that God would let them into Heaven. What a day of regret and despair that will be for so many people.

You may ask, "How can I be sure my name is written in the Book of Life?"

Jesus said, "Not everyone who says to me, 'Lord, Lord,'

will enter the kingdom of heaven, but only the one who does the will of my Father who is in heaven" (Matthew 7:21). What is the will of God the Father? His will is that we commit our lives to Jesus, that we confess that we are sinners, that we repent of our sins, and that receive Jesus, once and for all, as Lord and Savior. When you make that commitment, ask Jesus to write your name in his Book of Life. Then live every day in obedience and gratitude for the salvation and forgiveness he has freely given you.

Is your name written in the Book of Life?

Don't Delay

Don't wait another day, another moment. You don't know how much time remains. Through thousands of years, God has been patient with the human race. He has withheld his judgment and wrath, in spite of being cursed and hated and rejected by humanity. God's people have been persecuted by the ungodly, yet God has remained patient.

But don't assume he will be patient forever. One day his patience will come to an end. Jesus will come to judge the human race.

The contrast between Heaven and Hell could not be more stark. The time to prepare for the coming judgment is now. As Jesus said, "Keep watch because you do not know when the owner of the house will come back—whether in the evening, or at midnight, or when the rooster crows, or at dawn. If he comes suddenly, do not let him find you sleeping. What I say to you, I say to everyone: 'Watch!'" (Mark 13:35-37).

No one knows the day or the hour of the Lord's return. We must be vigilant and be ready for his return at any moment. How do you watch for his return? By obeying, by serving, by praying, by studying his Word, by remaining faithful to his commands.

Some people have said to me, "When things get really bad, I'll get right with God." Don't be fooled. This may be your one and only opportunity. Right now, you may be the nearest to Heaven you will ever be—and if you don't decide now, the moment of decision may never come again. Later, when you think you might be ready, you may have lost interest, or you may be gripped by unbreakable habits and addictions, or the people around you may cloud your thinking and lead you away from God.

Make sure you do not allow Satan to lull you into complacency and spiritual procrastination. Satan wants you to believe there's always more time to get right with God. He whispers, "You can make a decision for Christ tomorrow—there's no need to decide now." Beware of that kind of delusional thinking. It's a trap that Satan has set for you.

Decide now—and take your first step into Heaven. Your eternal life begins when you say "Yes" to Jesus. If you are ready to take that step, if you are ready to say *yes* to Jesus, then turn to page 197 and sincerely pray the prayer that is printed there. Then every day from here on out in gratitude for your salvation and in anticipation of Heaven.

With great excitement and expectation, we await the day of the Lord's return. It is a day that has long been promised in God's Word. It's a day that we long to see. When that day comes, our *real* life will begin.

No more pain. No more sorrow. No more bitterness. No more tears.

"Therefore keep watch," Jesus says. Be on guard. Don't fall asleep. Live each day as a citizen of Heaven.

That day is coming soon.

Prayer of Salvation

IF YOU HAVE NEVER surrendered your life to Jesus Christ, if you aren't sure that your name is written in the Book of Life, please pray this prayer now, in all sincerity:

Dear Lord Jesus, I have sinned against you. I am so sorry for my sin. I repent of my sin and ask you to forgive me. I know that you love me and that you died on the cross to save me. Have mercy on me, Lord, and blot out my sin. Make my heart clean. Write my name in your Book of Life with your own indelible blood. Fill me with your Holy Spirit. Help me to live faithfully every day out of gratitude to you. Thank you, Lord, for saving me. Thank you for the gift of eternal life in Heaven with you. Amen.

Notes

CHAPTER 1: HEAVEN IS ALL ABOUT JESUS

1. Randy Alcorn, *Heaven* (Wheaton, IL: Tyndale, 2004), 18.
2. Gene Barron, "Charles E. Fuller Once Announced That He Would Be . . . ," Sermon Central, January 19, 2002, https://www.sermoncentral.com/sermon-illustrations/5500/charles-e-fuller-once-announced-that-he-would-be-by-gene-barron.

CHAPTER 2: THE BEAUTY OF HEAVEN

1. D. L. Moody, *Heaven* (1900) (n.p.: Resurrected Press, 2014), 48.
2. Itzhak Bars and John Terning, *Extra Dimensions in Space and Time* (New York: Springer, 2010), 27.
3. John Henry Newman, "Holiness Necessary for Future Blessedness," in *Parochial and Plain Sermons*, vol. 1 (London: Longmans, Green, 1907), https://www.newmanreader.org/works/parochial/volume1/sermon1.html.
4. David Crosby, @thedavidcrosby, Twitter.com, Tweet: "I heard the place is overrated . . . cloudy," January 18, 2023, https://twitter.com/thedavidcrosby/status/1615681363600080899.
5. "Benjamin Franklin Epitaph, the" Historical Marker Database, accessed September 6, 2023, https://www.hmdb.org/m.asp?m=212552.
6. D. L. Moody, *Heaven: Where It Is and How to Get There* (Chicago: Fleming H. Revell, 1880), 20.

CHAPTER 3: THE BENEFITS OF HEAVEN

1. Adapted from Luis Palau, *Experiencing God's Forgiveness: Being Freed from Sin and Guilt* (Portland, OR: Multnomah, 1984).

2. You will find various examples of spiritual gifts in Romans 12, 1 Corinthians 12, Ephesians 4, and 1 Peter 4.

3. Paul Kroll, "Studies in the Book of Acts: Acts 21," Grace Communion International, 2012, https://learn.gcs.edu/mod/book/view.php?id=4475&chapterid=112; Ilan Ben Zion, "Ancient Temple Mount 'Warning' Stone Is 'Closest Thing We Have to the Temple'," *The Times of Israel*, October 22, 2015, https://www.timesofisrael.com/ancient-temple-mount-warning-stone-is-closest-thing-we-have-to-the-temple/.

4. Center for Human Rights in Iran, "Who Are the Dual and Foreign Nationals Imprisoned in Iran? (Updated)," IranHumanRights.org, May 24, 2018 (updated October 5, 2022), https://iranhumanrights.org/2018/05/who-are-the-dual-nationals-imprisoned-in-iran/.

CHAPTER 5: WHO GOES TO HEAVEN?

1. Isaac Asimov, *It's Been a Good Life*, ed. Janet Jeppson Asimov (Amherst, NY: Prometheus Books, 2002), 24–25.

2. Jerry F. Hough, *Changing Party Coalitions: The Mystery of the Red State-Blue State Alignment* (New York: Agathon Press, 2006), 203.

3. Ray C. Stedman, "Born of the Spirit," sermon at Peninsula Bible Church, Palo Alto, California, May 15, 1983; © 1983 by Ray Stedman Ministries. All rights reserved; https://www.raystedman.org/new-testament/john/born-of-the-spirit.

CHAPTER 6: THE THREE HEAVENS

1. Susan Zannos, *The Life and Times of Marco Polo* (Hockessin, DE: Mitchell Lane, 2005), 41.

2. Colonel Valentin Petrov, "Did Yuri Gagarin Say He Didn't See God in Space?" Pravmir.com, April 12, 2013, https://www.pravmir.com/did-yuri-gagarin-say-he-didnt-see-god-in-space; "Yuri Gagarin, First Human in Space, Was a Devout Christian, Says His Close Friend," Beliefnet.com, April 2011, https://www.beliefnet.com/columnists/on_the_front_lines_of_the_culture_wars/2011/04/yuri-gagarin-first-human-in-space-was-a-devout-christian-says-his-close-friend.html.

3. C. S. Lewis, *Mere Christianity* (New York: Macmillan, 1960), 118.

4. Veronika Kyrylenko, "Pornography in the Classroom? Sexually Explicit Material in Virginia Schools Sparks Outrage Among Parents," *The New American*, May 13, 2021, https://thenewamerican.com/us/education/pornography-in-the-classroom-sexually-explicit-material-in-virginia-schools-sparks-outrage-among-parents/.

5. Betsy McCaughey, "How Public Schools Brainwash Young Kids with Harmful Transgender Ideology," *New York Post*, December 22, 2021, https://nypost.com/2021/12/22/how-public-schools-brainwash-young -kids-with-harmful-transgender-ideology/; Emilie Kao, "Yes, Schools Are Secretly Trying to 'Gender Transition' Kids, and It Must Be Stopped," *The Daily Signal*, March 22, 2022, https://www.dailysignal.com/2022/03/22 /yes-schools-are-secretly-trying-to-gender-transition-kids-and-it-must-be -stopped/.

6. "Terry McAuliffe's War on Parents," *National Review*, October 1, 2021, https://www.nationalreview.com/2021/10/terry-mcauliffes-war-on -parents/; Ingrid Jacques, "Who Knows What's Best for Kids? Hint: Biden and Democrats Don't Think It's Parents," *USA Today*, April 27, 2023, https://www.usatoday.com/story/opinion/columnist/2023/04/27/biden -government-dictate-kids-education-schools-not-parents/11743676002/.

7. J. Irving Erickson, *Sing It Again!: A Handbook on the Covenant Hymnal* (Chicago: Covenant Press, 1985), 9–10.

8. Clifton Fadiman and André Bernard, eds., *Bartlett's Book of Anecdotes*, entry for "Beecher, Henry Ward" (Boston, MA: Little, Brown, 2000), 50.

9. See Psalm 115:16; Acts 7:49; Colossians 2:15; Revelation 20:1-3, 10.

CHAPTER 7: A NEW HEAVEN AND A NEW EARTH

1. David Guzik, "Revelation 21—A New Heavens, a New Earth, and a New Jerusalem," EnduringWord.com, 2019, https://enduringword.com/bible -commentary/revelation-21/.

2. Robert Lowry, "Shall We Gather at the River" (1864), public domain.

3. Adapted from "A Romance of Science and Devotion," *New Zealand Herald*, December 1, 1900, https://paperspast.natlib.govt.nz/newspapers /NZH19001201.2.66.10.

CHAPTER 8: ON EARTH AS IT IS IN HEAVEN

1. Adapted from Michael Youssef, *The Prayer that God Answers: Experience the Power and Fullness of the Lord's Prayer* (Nashville: Thomas Nelson, 2000), 41.

2. Randy Alcorn, *Heaven* (Wheaton, IL: Tyndale, 2004), 160.

3. C. S. Lewis, *The Magician's Nephew* (New York: HarperTrophy, 2000), 163.

4. Joni Eareckson Tada, *Heaven: Your Real Home . . . from a Higher Perspective* (Grand Rapids, MI: Zondervan, 1995, 2018), 152.

CHAPTER 9: WARNING! WARNING! WARNING!

1. CT Editors, "The 50 Countries Where It's Hardest to Follow Jesus in 2023," *Christianity Today*, https://www.christianitytoday.com/news/2023/january/christian-persecution-2023-countries-open-doors-watch-list.html.
2. Pastor Greg Laurie, "God, Drugs and Rock 'n' Roll: An Interview with Alice Cooper." YouTube.com, August 17, 2019, https://www.youtube.com/watch?v=k_GW7JL0-0k, 14:25–15:51.
3. Though this quote is often attributed to Nietzsche, it is not found in any of his published works.

About the Author

DR. MICHAEL YOUSSEF is a pastor, bestselling author, and internationally respected Bible teacher. Born in Egypt, he lived in Lebanon and Australia before coming to the United States and fulfilling a childhood dream of becoming an American citizen. He founded The Church of The Apostles in Atlanta in 1987, and the church became the launching pad for *Leading The Way with Dr. Michael Youssef,* an international media ministry that now reaches audiences in nearly every major city in the world. His Middle Eastern heritage, keen understanding of Christian worldview issues, and unwavering passion for the gospel have given Dr. Youssef the unique ability to speak boldly into today's issues. He has authored more than fifty books, including popular titles *Saving Christianity?, Life-Changing Prayers, Hope for This Present Crisis, Never Give Up,* and his latest book, *Is the End Near?* He and his wife reside in Atlanta and have four grown children and thirteen grandchildren.